CORONATION
June 2 1953

CONRAD FROST

CORONATION
June 2 1953

Arthur Barker Limited
London

for Brandi

Contents

Acknowledgements

Illustrations are reproduced by kind permission of the following: Bippa: 15 (b); Camera Press: 53; Dean and Chapter of Westminster: 63 (b); Fox Photos: 13 (t), 49 (b), 68 (b), 70 (b), 83 (b), 120, 137 (b), 145, 146; London Express: 5, 7 (b), 23 (t & b), 27 (b), 31, 47 (b), 49 (t), 57 (t & b), 68 (t), 73 (b), 75, 77 (b), 88, 89, 93, 97, 99, 101, 104, 106, 109, 117, 133 (b); Mary Evans Picture Library: 29 (b); Popperfoto: 13 (b), 15 (t), 19 (t & b), 25, 27 (t), 36, 40 (t & b), 43 (t & b), 47 (t), 55, 59 (t & b), 60, 63 (t), 70 (t), 72 (t & b), 73 (t), 77 (t), 79, 81, 83 (t), 85, 90, 94, 103 (t & b), 108, 110, 113, 115, 119, 123, 125, 126 (t & b), 127, 129 (t & b), 130, 133 (t), 134, 137 (t), 140, 141, 143, 144 (t & b), 149, 150; *Punch*: 7 (t).

Colour illustrations are reproduced by kind permission of the following: State Coach: Fox Photos; Crown Jewels: Crown Copyright reproduced by kind permission of the Controller of Her Majesty's Stationery Office; Queen leaving Palace: Woodmansterne; Churchill: Woodmansterne; Admiralty Arch: Fox Photos; Queen Mother: Woodmansterne; Queen crowned: Fox Photos; back to Palace: Woodmansterne; waving: Woodmansterne.

Author's Note

I FIRST THOUGHT TO write this book in 1953, when I was working for Lord Kemsley. At that time I was responsible for an heterogeneous supply of features material to the Kemsley regional and national newspapers. Because it was spending dollars to 'buy wholesale' from the American syndication market, my set-up became temporarily satellite to Ian Fleming's Foreign Department.

Fleming involved me that year in finding an artist, Ken Lewis, to do the jacket for a book he had written, but about which he had no great expectations. It was the first James Bond novel, *Casino Royale*. He was indirectly responsible, also, for sidetracking me from tackling my own book project for that year.

I had produced and offered to the regional morning papers of the Group what was intended to be a short-run daily text and illustration feature digesting the history of the reign of the first Queen Elizabeth. We launched the feature under the title 'An Age of Greatness'.

Fleming, in a moment of characteristic enthusiasm, drew Lord Kemsley's attention to the first week's publications. Kemsley, who was an autocrat, immediately ordered that his regional newspapers should cease publication forthwith.

At this time both the circulation and the revenues of the *Daily Graphic* were plunging. Kemsley, shortly to sell the paper to Lord Rothermere, was giving it priority with every idea he thought worthwhile. He took Fleming's judgment as sound and Henry Clapp, editor of the *Graphic*, was told to re-run the opening week. 'An Age of Greatness' was now to have a six months run and I had a major research, writing and production job on my hands. By the time it was over, it was too late to write the book and anyway, my moment of enthusiasm was over.

Twenty-five years later has been a better time to write it. History should be recorded objectively and from a little distance. It is not that the facts become different, only that what they were becomes recognizable.

1

The Road to the Throne

THE YEAR 1936 WAS known as 'the year of the three kings'. At the beginning of that year the nine-year-old Princess Elizabeth Alexandra Mary had not seemed a likely future queen. Too many possibilities stood between her and her accession. By the end of that year a flood of events had made it probable that she would one day be queen of England.

Only twice before had England had three successive kings in the same year. Inevitably such circumstances must be momentous in the history of the monarchy. They are also likely to be disruptive to the line of direct succession. It had happened in 1066 after the Norman invasion. It had happened in 1483 as a consequence of the murder of the 'princes in the Tower'. It happened again in 1936 as the result of a man's infatuation for a woman.

In that year Princess Elizabeth's grandfather, King George V, died on 20 January. The popular Prince of Wales, her uncle David (the name by which he was known to everyone), succeeded as Edward VIII, but the coronation planned for him never took place. Instead, after a reign of only ten months and twenty-one days, her uncle abdicated so that he could marry a divorced American commoner, Mrs Wallis Simpson. Elizabeth's father, the Duke of York, was proclaimed King George VI.

A brief, single-page document, the Instrument of Abdication, signed at Edward's home, Fort Belvedere, two days previously, announced his 'irrevocable determination to renounce the Throne for Myself and for My descendants. . . .' With her father now king, Elizabeth became heir-presumptive to the throne – but not heir-apparent because, being a girl, she was heir only upon the continuing presumption that no male heir would be born to her parents, to take precedence over her. But that presumption was a strong and well-founded one. The new King's family was very much regarded as complete – the Queen was now thirty-seven, and there is reliable evidence that the entire royal family took it for granted that there would be no further children. In many ways the new King – a quiet, reserved family man – was a more suitable occupant of the throne than his pleasure-loving elder brother.

Some months before his death, when the Prince of Wales' *affaire* with Mrs Simpson was becoming public knowledge, George v, who had never been on good terms with his eldest son, is reported as having said: 'I pray to God that my eldest son will never marry and have children and that nothing will come between Bertie [the Duke of York] and Lilibet [Princess Elizabeth] and the throne.'

1934 was the fateful year. For, by this time, although the general public in the United Kingdom had never heard of the lady, Edward's infatuation for Mrs Wallis Simpson created a volcanic situation. The Prince of Wales seemed hell-bent on challenging everyone from his father down to the press to accept Mrs Simpson. She was seen everywhere with him – at parties, at night clubs, at country house weekends. And as if wishing to emphasize his infatuation for her, he showered her with jewellery. It was breathtaking, not merely because £50,000's worth of jewellery was followed up by £60,000's worth a week later, but because of the impudence of the challenge to his family. Much of the jewellery was bought for her by the Prince, but he also gave her, and she wore, the emeralds which Queen Alexandra had personally left to him to be worn by his future wife.

With hindsight one may now see the significance of Mrs Wallis Simpson 'dripping with emeralds', as Sir Henry Channon was to describe her in his diaries of the period – the emeralds one Queen of England had intended that another Queen should wear. The Prince of Wales' future wife *was* wearing them, although at the time nobody had the imagination or the foresight to see that he already had every intention of marrying her, come what might.

King George and Queen Mary had never been naive about their eldest son's affairs with women. They clearly deplored and disapproved of standards lower than those they felt it was the duty of themselves and their family to set to other people. But undoubtedly they, like the politicians, believed that in due course Edward would settle down and come to terms with making a suitable marriage and providing an heir to the throne. But, while they had ignored his previous affairs, it was different in the case of Wallis Simpson, parading herself in public wearing Queen Alexandra's emeralds. This was bitterly hurtful, especially to Queen Mary. Even the rest of the family clearly thought that Edward was going too far this time, though it would seem that his brothers and sisters had had a certain admiration for the way in which Edward had refused to be moulded into the pattern of dull, conventional morality, and they had accepted his mistresses. Mrs Simpson was different, and they seemed to sense that.

Late that year there were reports of an incident that substantiate the idea that this time Edward was determined upon recognition for his future wife and not his present mistress. A ball was being held at Buckingham Palace as a prelude to the wedding of Prince George and Princess Marina. When the guest list was being prepared, Edward put in the names of Mr and Mrs Ernest Simpson. When it was submitted to George V for his approval he crossed out those two names.

The matter was out into the open. Unfortunately, the evidence is conflicting and lacks adequate authentification to judge what really was said between the King and his son. One account is that Edward told his father that he must stand for the principle that his friends should be welcomed at the Palace, and that if any guests of his choosing were vetoed, then he himself would not attend the ball. The other account is that George V challenged his son with the gossip that Mrs Simpson was his mistress, and that Edward gave the assurance that she was not.

Whatever the truth, Edward got his way, the Simpsons did attend the ball and Wallis was presented to King George V and Queen Mary – a brief, formal and impersonal introduction and the only meeting she was ever to have with her future husband's parents.

Throughout 1935 the 'Wallis Simpson affair' developed slowly and inevitably, but still off-stage. There was, anyway, much to distract attention from the Prince of Wales. There was the Duke of Kent's wedding to Princess Marina, there was King George V's Silver Jubilee and finally the wedding of the Duke of Gloucester to Lady Alice Montagu-Douglas-Scott.

During this year, however, there was a development that was possibly more worrying to the politicians than the affair with Mrs Simpson. The Prince had not concealed the fact that he approved of Hitler and Mussolini and that he did not see the Fascist dictatorships as representing a threat to the United Kingdom. It was embarrassing that, at a British Legion rally, he made these personal views quite clear. It was ominous that Mrs Simpson should be a guest at a German Embassy dinner party. These things worried the government because, although the British press discreetly ignored them, both the German and American press interpreted them as being indicative of a political government attitude. One of the debatable factors about the abdication crisis will always remain the question of to what degree, if any, Edward's dangerous and embarrassing political sympathies may have influenced the course of events.

By the end of 1935 it began to be predictable that George V's reign did not have much longer to run. He was seventy and was suffering badly from the bronchial trouble that had never really left him since his grave illness in 1928. The few people who were fully aware of the situation took comfort from the hope that, faced now with the realities of being king, Edward would come to his senses. Indeed it was almost unthinkable to consider anything else. Instead there was almost instant evidence after George v's death that, far from being over, the curtain was only just rising on the drama.

One of the first traditional rituals of an accession is the reading of the Proclamation of Accession by the Garter King of Arms from the balcony of St James's Palace. Edward made arrangements to watch the ceremony from the windows of a room in the Palace, overlooking Friary Court. Among the guests, establishing the fact that the King's accession was to make no difference to her role in his life, was Mrs Simpson. By an unfortunate chance, as she and Edward were close to a window and together, a photographer got a picture in which the King could be seen to be exhausted while, at that moment, Mrs Simpson was laughing. There could have been no more unpropitious curtain raiser to the reign than that photograph, taken out of the context of a roomful of guests and, by a cruel chance of mistiming, satirizing the relationship even before most people knew that it existed. Such pictures, however, found their publication abroad and not in the United Kingdom where the newspapers maintained their self-imposed conspiracy of silence.

The new King himself, on the other hand, had no intention of leading any kind of double life. He told Lord Monckton, his principle adviser, that if they wanted a monarch like his father, there was always the Duke of York. And he wanted a wife, not a mistress. The issue about his eventual marriage to the woman he loved had to be settled before the coronation, which was arranged for 12 May the following year. He would not go through that ceremony with a secret determination in his mind to marry contrary to the Church's tenets. And he deplored discretion as being, in this situation, a form of dishonesty.

The first two months of the reign were uneventful. Later it was to be remarked that Edward seemed to have been much more emotionally upset than other members of the royal family. From this retrospective observation arose a theory in which there could be some truth. It was that the Prince had for some time been considering the possibility of renouncing his right to the succession, but no moment had been right to take this step. Now he found himself trapped by events. He had left it too late.

In March, Hitler broke the Locarno Pact and German troops reoccupied the Rhineland. Von Neurath, the German Foreign Minister, reported that

The instrument of abdication, signed by Edward and his three brothers, The Dukes of York, Gloucester and Kent.

INSTRUMENT OF ABDICATION

I, Edward the Eighth, of Great
Britain, Ireland, and the British Dominions
beyond the Seas, King, Emperor of India, do
hereby declare My irrevocable determination
to renounce the Throne for Myself and for
My descendants, and My desire that effect
should be given to this Instrument of
Abdication immediately.

In token whereof I have hereunto set
My hand this tenth day of December, nineteen
hundred and thirty six, in the presence of
the witnesses whose signatures are subscribed.

SIGNED AT
FORT BELVEDERE
IN THE PRESENCE
OF

Edward RI

Albert

Henry.

George.

the King was opposed to any British intervention and that he was in sympathy with both German and Italian aspirations. A secret Italian despatch to Berlin reported upon a private meeting in London between the King and Snr Grandi, the Italian ambassador, in May, in which Edward said that the British Government's backing of the League of Nations' move to enforce economic sanctions against Italy could be dismissed.

This evidence of what were indiscretions of misjudgment on the King's part was not found until after the war but already, in the spring of that year, Stanley Baldwin had come to the conclusion that the King was not to be trusted with policy and security secrets. It was unconstitutional, but from about that time there was a secret censorship of the documents sent to him.

In May Mrs Simpson took the first secret steps towards obtaining a divorce. At about the same time, Edward was responsible for the inclusion of her name in Court Circulars publishing dinner party guest lists. At such a party, at which Mr Simpson was significantly not present, Mrs Simpson was a fellow guest of the Duke and Duchess of York, of Winston Churchill and his wife and of Sir Samuel Hoare. Quite clearly the King was using other members of the royal family and distinguished politicians and their wives to establish a background of acceptance of Mrs Simpson. But by doing this he was, in fact, contributing to the growing resentment of her.

On 27 October Mrs Simpson was granted a decree nisi at the Ipswich Assizes. The grounds for the divorce related to an occasion of adultery between her husband and a lady named Buttercup Kennedy.

Shortly afterwards, Prime Minister Baldwin went to the King on his own initiative to tell him that constitutional issues were now becoming involved and that the situation was becoming damaging to the very foundations of the Monarchy. Events were to justify this move as not untimely. Before the year was out the commons were to be voting on a motion that the crown should be replaced by 'government of a Republican kind'.

In November, the King's Private Secretary, Alexander Hardinge, made a written report in which he warned the King that the silence of the British press could not be maintained much longer. He predicted the inevitability of crisis and recommended that Mrs Simpson should leave the country at once. For the King himself, this was the moment of confrontation.

By 16 November Edward had made up his mind. He saw Baldwin again and he told him: 'I am going to marry Mrs Simpson, and I am prepared to go.' He dined with Queen Mary and for the first time told his mother of his feelings for Mrs Simpson.

On 20 November Baldwin was seen again to discuss the possibility of

A typical cartoon which appeared in *Punch* at the time of the abdication crisis.

THE CHOICE

THE PRIME MINISTER. "ALL THE PEOPLES OF YOUR EMPIRE, SIR, SYMPATHISE WITH YOU MOST DEEPLY; BUT THEY ALL KNOW—AS YOU YOURSELF MUST—THAT THE THRONE IS GREATER THAN THE MAN."

The Duke and Duchess of Windsor after the wedding ceremony in France on 3 June 1937.

Parliament passing a special bill that would allow the King to marry Mrs Simpson without her becoming Queen and without any children she might have having any claim to the throne. But on 2 December, after a cabinet meeting, the Prime Minister went to see the King and, during a seventy-five-minute meeting, told him that, although enquiries were not yet completed, it was already clear that neither the British Parliament, nor the Dominions, would tolerate a morganatic marriage.

Edward now had three clear choices. He could keep the throne and give up Mrs Simpson. Constitutionally, he could ask for Baldwin's resignation, and rule with a new cabinet – and he would have found some support for this course. Or he could abdicate.

Now arose the real issue as far as Princess Elizabeth's ultimate succession to the throne was concerned. Although he was not ready to make it known, Edward's decision was already made. It was not, however, one that would necessarily make Elizabeth a future queen. It was not a legal necessity that, if Edward abdicated, his successor should be next in hereditary order for Parliament could be asked, in exactly the same way as it had been asked to approve a morganatic marriage, to change the laws of succession. That this possibility created a crisis within a crisis was not revealed at the time, but later those close to events were to suggest that the idea of transferring the succession to the Duke of Kent, who already had a son who could have become the Prince of Wales, was seriously considered. The Duke of York's speech defect had been an agonizing embarrassment to him all his life. He had faced up to it and sought to overcome it with a personal courage that stamps him quite simply as a brave man. Nevertheless, although the Duke had undertaken his full share of public duties, there was inevitable anxiety as to whether it was not asking too much of him to undertake the strenuous and difficult role of monarch. To what varying degrees, if any, the politicians, members of the royal family, the King and even the Duke himself may have been involved in this thinking will never be known.

On the morning of 3 December the newspapers had broken the news that the King wanted to marry the twice-divorced American, Mrs Simpson, and that there was a state of crisis between him and the cabinet. On that same Thursday the King rang the Duke of York and asked him to come to Fort Belvedere the next morning.

On Friday, 4 December, Mr Baldwin went to Fort Belvedere, but when the Duke of York rang to confirm his appointment, he was put off until the next day. On Saturday, 5 December the cabinet met in the morning.

Walter Monckton, the King's legal adviser, spent two hours at No. 10 Downing Street. He then went to Fort Belvedere. Mr Baldwin went to Fort Belvedere. That afternoon Walter Monckton formally told Stanley Baldwin of the King's definite decision to abdicate. But when the Duke of York rang his brother, Edward said: 'I will see you and tell you my decision when I have made up my mind. Come and see me on Sunday.'

On Sunday, 6 December, Walter Monckton, who knew of the abdication decision, was at 10 Downing Street at 9.15 in the morning. At ten o'clock, Mr Baldwin, who also now knew of the decision, began a conference of ministers. The conference was presently adjourned, and Mr Baldwin went to Marlborough House to see Queen Mary. When he returned, the conference was resumed. Meanwhile, the Duke of York, who had been told nothing of these events, eventually rang Fort Belvedere in the evening and was told that the King was in conference and would call back. There was no telephone call that evening.

The next day the Duke of York waited until after lunch and then rang the King. Edward said that he might be able to see him that evening. It was not until six hours later that Edward finally called and said: 'Come and see me.'

Even more significant than the fact that the King did not inform his presumed successor of the abdication decision until two days after he had announced it to the Prime Minister was that during this critical period neither Baldwin, nor Walter Monckton, nor any other involved politician or negotiator had any communication with the man who was legally the successor to the throne.

When the newspapers broke the news of the situation on 3 December, reactions were violent. Extremists threw bricks through Mrs Simpson's windows. Oswald Mosley's blackshirts marched through the East End in support of the King. Someone tried to throw vitriol in Mrs Simpson's face. She left the country to join friends at the Villa Lou Viei in Cannes. And from that moment Edward's abdication was certain.

It was not, however, until 10 December that, an agreed Instrument of Abdication having been prepared for his signature, he took the course that meant that, sixteen years later, Elizabeth would be Queen. On the Leader Page of the *Daily Sketch* for Friday, 11 December, 1936, the feature article was a pen-picture of the ten-year-old princess. 'Unless a son is born to her parents,' it said, 'England, after three centuries, will one day again be ruled by an Elizabeth.' That was the day on which the throne became Elizabeth's destiny.

2

The State of the Nation

ON FRIDAY, 11 DECEMBER 1936, a letter was delivered to 145, Piccadilly, addressed to 'Her Majesty the Queen'. It lay on the hall table where Princess Elizabeth saw it. 'That's mummy now, isn't it,' she said to Lady Cynthia Asquith, a visitor. The heir presumptive to the throne, whose weekly pocket money was one shilling (5p), and whose sole ambition at the moment was to gain her life-saving certificate, had not been unaware of the drama taking place around her. From now on the Princess' education was to be directed towards an objective understanding of both domestic and international events and political situations.

Sixteen years later, when Elizabeth became Queen, the physical scars of the Second World War still seared the blitzed cities. Austerity was not over, and food rationing was still being endured; it was a very different Britain from that of 1936. But the 1951 Festival of Britain had already been recognized as the milestone of a new era.

The Festival commemorated the centenary of the Great Exhibition of 1851 and, at the time, the whole project seemed disastrous in conception and likely to be so in accomplishment. To begin with the planning of a celebration seemed mistimed when the casualty lists of dead and wounded were coming in from the Imjin river in Korea.

Then the King, who had recovered from his operation in 1949 for arteriosclerosis – a form of thrombosis in which circulation through the leg arteries is restricted – was now unwell again. There had been tentative plans for a Royal procession up river from the Tower to the South Bank Exhibition site in the State barge for the dedication ceremonial on 3 May. Instead there was a service at St Paul's Cathedral. The King looked both tired and ill.

And Attlee's Labour Government, which had to pay the piper for the Festival, was tired and ill, too. Bevan had split the party by resigning on the issue of National Health Service charges.

The whole of Gerald Barry's plan for a National 'tonic' of 'fun, fantasy and colour' ran into budget problems as critics campaigned against the alleged extravagance of the South Bank Skylon, the Dome of Discovery and the Battersea Park pleasure gardens.

Architecturally the South Bank buildings offended the aesthetic taste of the traditionalists whose verdict on the one permanent building, the Royal Festival Hall, was to be that it was ugly. Strikes added to the problems, and the South Bank Exhibition was incomplete when the Festival began.

It was, nevertheless, an enormous success. That summer, over eight million people visited the South Bank and the Festival Gardens at Battersea. But when the Festival closed in September, the King was not well enough to be there for the song sung by Gracie Fields that brought the curtain down on an event which the war-wearied, austerity-weary public had turned to as a diversion.

The King's illness was serious. Soon after the opening of the Festival of Britain, he had had an attack of influenza. His recovery was so slow that a leading chest surgeon, Clement Price Thomas, was called in, ostensibly to examine a chronic bronchial trouble.

The King had cancer. It was necessary to remove one lung despite the fact that, with the previous history of thrombosis, there was a high risk of a coronary attack either during the operation or in the days immediately following. Certain nerves of the larynx had to be removed with the consequential possibility that he might never be able to speak again above a whisper.

They told him only that there was a bronchial tube blockage. He never knew the truth – or if he suspected it he entered bravely into the conspiracy of silence that helps to make such situations a little more bearable.

The operation took place on 23 September, but its success was only a respite. Meanwhile Attlee had decided to accept the challenge that Opposition tactics were forcing on him and to go the country. The polling date was set for 21 October.

The country put Churchill back in power, although the majority, twice as large as Attlee had had, was far from comfortable. The Conservatives had 321 seats, Labour 295, Liberals 6, others, 3.

Although the King conferred the Order of Merit on Attlee, and saw Churchill to discuss senior cabinet appointments, he was too ill to receive the retiring and incoming Ministers. And that November the King's Speech was read for him by the Lord Chancellor.

Too many people have lived with the situation that George VI's family were living with for understanding to depend upon explanation. When

Princess Elizabeth and the Duke of Edinburgh left for a postponed Canadian tour on 7 October, with them in their luggage went a prepared accession declaration, and the formal messages to both Houses of Parliament that would have to be made if her father died during their ninety-five-day tour. Ironically, when they got back they discovered that apparently the only worry the King had was that his new Prime Minister, Winston Churchill, was over seventy-five, had had a stroke, and had become a little slow in his movements and slurred in his speech.

The King himself was only fifty-six that month. He celebrated his birthday with the family, quietly, at Buckingham Palace, and then, on December 21, went to Sandringham for Christmas.

The traditional King's Broadcast had always been the cause of a shadow of anxious anticipation for him, but this year, for the first time, the hoarseness of his throat after the operation, and his post-operative weakness meant that he was not expected to even try to make a live speech. He pre-recorded his speech in short sessions, and it was then edited into the whole he was able to listen to after lunch, with the family.

Princess Elizabeth and the Duke of Edinburgh were due to make an official tour of Britain's East African possession, leaving on 31 January 1952. The tour was to take in Australia and New Zealand. It is improbable that it was merely coincidental that the King was due to have a medical check-up on 29 January. His doctors were satisfied with the progress of his recovery.

The next evening, for the first time since his operation, the royal family had an evening out as a farewell to the young couple the next day. They went to see *South Pacific* at Drury Lane. It was their last family party together and that, whatever the doctors might optimistically have said, was a possibility that must have been in the mind of Princess Elizabeth.

The next day was a cold day of strong winds. The King insisted on going to Heathrow to say goodbye to his daughter and son-in-law. The last pictures taken of him were as he stood bareheaded on the tarmac, in the wind, his hand lifted in the gesture of farewell.

From Heathrow he went to Sandringham where a small party of friends were waiting for him for a shooting party. They had a good weekend and it stretched over into the following week. On Tuesday, 5 February, they were a party of seven ranging over the land of the King's oldest tenant, George Brereton of Flitcham Hall. One of the guns was Lord Fermoy, whose land adjoined the King's at Sandringham, and who had been a friend for twenty-seven years.

The quarry was hare, and at the end of the morning the huntsmen had

After his coronation, George VI
waves to the crowds with his
wife, the young Princesses and
his mother, Queen Mary.

George VI waves goodbye to
Princess Elizabeth and the Duke
of Edinburgh at London
Airport. The young couple were
flying to Kenya for the first stage
of their Commonwealth tour: it
was the last time the Princess
was to see her father.

shot 280. They went back to Sandringham for lunch, and the King spent an hour watching Lord Fermoy teaching his grandson, Prince Charles, to skate on the frozen lake in front of the house.

It looked as if the crisp, clear weather was now going to hold and so they planned another shoot not on the next day, but the day after:

'Well, Maurice,' the King said to Lord Fermoy when they parted, 'I'll see you on Thursday at about the same time.'

On the evening of Tuesday, 5 February, he stayed up with the Queen and Princess Margaret to hear the ten o'clock news on the radio, and went to his bedroom an hour later. A footman took him a cup of hot chocolate and he read until about midnight when a watchman in the garden saw him fastening the latch of his bedroom window.

At seven-thirty the next morning, the assistant valet took him his usual cup of tea. But when the curtains were opened, the King did not move. He had died, during the night, of a coronary thrombosis.

Under the Succession Act of 1707, Elizabeth became the sovereign the moment her father died, and she is the only British sovereign in modern history whose moment of accession is unknown. She was also the first sovereign in more than 200 years to accede to the British throne while abroad – it had last happened when George I, who had been in Hanover when Queen Anne died, became King in 1714.

The only precise historical fact known about the moment of the accession of Queen Elizabeth II is that she was in a hut built in the branches of a giant fig tree overlooking a wild animal waterhole in Africa. The royal couple were staying in the Treetops Hotel in Kenya when the first reports of the King's death started coming in.

Martin Charteris, the Princess' Private Secretary, was away from Treetops making preparations for the next stage of the tour. A reporter from the *East African Standard* contacted him urgently, and said: 'I've just had a call from my office in Nairobi. The King is dead. They got it on the Reuter wire.' The news was immediately telephoned to the Duke of Edinburgh's Private Secretary. It was difficult to obtain confirmation because a violent tropical thunderstorm was making telephone communications practically inaudible, and there was nobody at Government House in Nairobi who could decode the cipher telegrams that were now coming in.

At 2.45 pm local time Princess Elizabeth was in the sitting-room of the Sagana hunting lodge with the Duke of Edinburgh. She did not see Michael Parker, the Duke's Private Secretary, urgently beckoning to the Duke

At Nyeri, in Kenya, on 6 February 1952, the question of a 'correct' signature for the new Queen arose. Elizabeth Alexandra Mary, the only expert on constitutional law in that country, decided correctly that this was how she should now sign herself.

The young Queen arriving at London Airport from Kenya on hearing the tragic news of her father's death.

through the bay window. The news had by now been confirmed, and the Duke was left to tell his wife that her father had died and that she was the Queen.

The time for private grief was not now. The prepared documentation of inheritance that Major Charteris now arranged for her signature was part of the standard equipment that always travelled with her.

While the Duke involved himself with the arrangements for an immediate return to England, Elizabeth began the first formalities of her reign. She had to write personal messages to her mother, her sister, Queen Mary and the Duke of Gloucester. Then, herself, she drafted telegrams to her hosts in Australia and New Zealand, not cancelling but postponing her visits.

Direct contact with London was now established and there was a formal request from Winston Churchill for permission to call a meeting of the Accession Council. Answering it posed her with the first personal decision of her reign – how she should sign herself. Should she sign herself 'Elizabeth R' – the 'R' standing for Regina – before the Accession Council proclaimed her the Queen? There was no expert upon constitutional law in Kenya other than herself. 'I sign it Elizabeth R,' she decided, and was right.

Meanwhile the Prince found that the Air Force, the Navy and BOAC had already moved into action and that an intricate and complex operation was being mounted to get the Queen from Kenya to London quickly and safely. And the whole operation was dependent on the Queen leaving Nyeri at five o'clock.

The problem was that the nearest airfield was a bush landing strip forty-five miles away at Nanyuki, on the Equator. The BOAC Argonaut *Atlanta*, which had brought the royal party to Kenya, was now at Mombasa. Nanyuki's runway was too short for the big four-engine airliner, so an East African Airways Dakota would have to be used to fly the Queen from Nanyuki to Entebbe in Uganda where the Argonaut would rendezvous. The Nanyuki take-off had to be before 7 pm, when it would be dark, because Nanyuki had no flare-path.

There was time for what was to be the Queen's first meeting with any of her subjects – among them Waithaka, of the Kikuyu tribe, the butler; and Juma, the Swahili houseboy; and the Somali table boy, Hussein. For them, and all the household and game staff, there were the already prepared souvenir gifts of cuff-links, fountain pens and cigarette lighters. The photographs had to be autographed, the first to be so, with the new signature – 'Elizabeth R'. There was a personal word of thanks to each of them, and the first handshakes of the reign. As she left the Lodge, the Askari troops, whose tents were in the grounds, and who had been on guard, presented arms, giving the first royal salute to the new sovereign. Across all the centuries of the monarchy there had been no more unusual accession.

After a twenty-four-hour journey from Africa, the Queen's plane landed at Heathrow in conditions of low cloud. As it touched down, a police motorcycle escort raced out to the runway to lead the way back to the tarmac, the waiting politicians and her uncle, the Duke of Gloucester. It was just after five o'clock in London when the Royal Standard broke out over over Clarence House to indicate that the Queen was home for the first time. For Bernard Marmaduke Fitzalan-Howard, 16th Duke of Norfolk, Earl Marshal of England, the role of impresario-extraordinary now began. As Earl Marshal he would be responsible for the new Queen's coronation.

3

In Accordance with Tradition

IN SHAKESPEARE's *Richard III*, Thomas Howard, Duke of Norfolk, has a very minor, five-line role to play in the battlefield scenes in which the King is slain. In fact he had been responsible for the coronation of 'unsanctioned usurpation' of Richard, Duke of Gloucester, when Richard claimed the throne in 1483. Lord Howard, as he then was, had been seated at the new King's right hand in Westminster Hall where thirty-five peers of England and seventy of her knights accepted Richard instead of the boy king, Edward v, who was by now a prisoner in the Tower. To show his gratitude, Richard granted Lord Howard the appointment of Earl Marshal, to be responsible for all principal state ceremonies, including coronations. The reward for this service was, traditionally, 'the horse and palfrey on which the king rode to his place of coronation, together with the bridles, saddles and caparisons; also the cloth spread at the table whereat the king dined; the cloth of estate which hung behind the king at dinner; the chines of all swans and cranes served up, and sundry other fees appertinent to the office of High Usher.' Later an honorarium of £20 a year was substituted for these 'perks', and that sum has never been increased. The Catholic dukes of Norfolk had held the appointment for nearly 500 years, occasionally relegating it to Protestant relatives in times of danger.

The 16th Duke already had some personal experience of being in charge of what is, unquestionably, the most spectacular event in the world, with a cast of thousands to organize and with responsibility for the most valuable 'props' ever assembled for public exhibition. At the age of twenty-nine, in 1937, he had been responsible for a coronation he had begun to plan for one king but at which another had been crowned. Although the date for Queen Elizabeth's coronation was sixteen months ahead, all that time was needed for planning and preparation.

The ceremony in early times had been a very simple one. Its origins go back

The Queen's first Christmas Day broadcast to the Commonwealth from Sandringham.

The 16th Duke of Norfolk, Earl Marshal of England, seen here against his banner, had already organized one coronation when it became his responsibility to arrange for the coronation of Elizabeth II. In 1483 his ancestor, Lord Howard, had organized the coronation of Richard III.

to the days when an elected European chief was hoisted on a shield and carried round on the shoulders of the strongest men of his tribe as a ceremony of recognition. Known as the *gyratio*, the shield-carrying ritual survived in the Roman Empire for many centuries, gradually developing from a proclamation of accession to the beginnings of a crowning or coronation. One of the most fully reported of such ceremonies took place in AD 565 when the Emperor Justinian died. Members of the senate, anxious to avoid the civil war that would have developed if all seven of Justinian's nephews – each already in a position of high command and with armed followers – disputed the succession, made their own choice. At midnight a deputation of senators awakened the Emperor's nephew Justin with the news that his uncle was dead and that he had been chosen to succeed. Justin was hurried to the palace where he was put into the imperial garments – red buskins, white tunic, purple robe and a diadem of richly embossed linen. This, the actual coronation ceremony, was in fact only a prelude to what really mattered. He was then carried, standing, on a shield borne by four of the royal guards, to the Hippodrome. Here he was exhibited to be acclaimed by the assembled crowd. Justin made certain of his undisputed succession in a very practical way. He was followed into the Hippodrome by porters carrying bags of gold. This gold was distributed, on the spot, to his uncle's many creditors – who might otherwise have despaired of repayment.

The role of the senators on this particular occasion was similar to that played by the Witan, or council of elders, of the Anglo-Saxons. It survives in Britain in the form of the Accession Council. The Witan, in their day, had simply chosen the man they thought most suitable to be the new king. They, in their turn, were replaced by the Great Council of the Norman kings. The Great Council, although it observed the principle of hereditary descent, did not always follow it except in a general way. Indeed, after the Conquest, five of the first six kings rested their principal title upon being the elected choice of the people. When Richard Coeur de Lion died, with no other direct heir beyond an illegitimate son, Philip, his twelve-year-old nephew, Arthur, had already been declared the heir-apparent. But the Great Council, held at Northampton, elected John in preference. At the coronation at Westminster on 25 May 1199, the Archbishop of Canterbury opened the ceremony with one of the most remarkable public speeches ever made on an occasion of this kind, his intention being to justify the exclusion of the heir-apparent. The crown, he said, was not the property of any particular person. It was the gift of the nation and the nation chose, generally, from members of the reigning family, the prince who appeared to be the most deserving of royalty in the existing circumstances.

Until 1867 the Council, which was composed of officers of state and prelates and barons, had powers beyond those of Parliament which, before that year, became immediately dissolved upon the death of a monarch. It was after 1869 that Parliament began to legislate in matters affecting the crown. Nevertheless, following tradition, when Parliament assembled on the afternoon of 6 February 1952, after members had taken the oath of allegiance to the new monarch, the politicians retired and left the stage to the Accession Privy Council.

The Privy Council nowadays consists of members of the royal family, cabinet ministers, the archbishops and the Bishop of London, the officers of state, the Lord Chancellor, the chief judges, the Speaker of the House of Commons, the First Lord of the Admiralty, and Commonwealth Prime Ministers and High Commissioners. It may also include anyone nominated by the sovereign provided they are natural-born British subjects. There were more than 300 Privy Councillors in England alone, to receive summonses by hand if they were in London, or by telegram if they were not, to attend the Accession Privy Council at St James's Palace at five o'clock that evening. Their task was to sign the proclamation that:

We, the Lords spiritual and temporal of this realm being here assisted with these his late Majesty's Privy Council, with representatives of other members of the Commonwealth, with other principal gentlemen of quality, with the Lord Mayor, aldermen and citizens of London, do now hereby with one voice and consent of tongue and heart publish and proclaim:

The high and mighty Princess Elizabeth Alexandra Mary is now by the death of our late Sovereign of happy memory become Queen Elizabeth the Second by the Grace of God. Queen of this realm and of her other realms and territories, head of the Commonwealth, Defender of the Faith.

There were 150 people attending the ceremony, including the deputy Prime Minister of Australia who happened to be in Paris and who chartered a plane in order to be present. The Council clerk read the prepared proclamation which was different from those used for the three previous proclamations of accession. The words 'the Crown' had been substituted for the previous 'the Imperial Crown of Great Britain, Ireland and all other of his late Majesty's Dominions'. The words 'Head of the Commonwealth' instead of 'British Dominions beyond the seas' were new. For the first time since Victoria had been proclaimed Empress of India, this reference was eliminated.

The meeting lasted only twenty minutes. By tradition the new sovereign should now have entered the hall and made a formal declaration of resolve, taken the oath to 'preserve the settlement of the true Protestant religion as established by laws made in Scotland', and then signed two copies of the declaration, one for immediate despatch to Edinburgh. At that moment, however, the new Queen was 4,200 miles away on the forty-five-mile journey along rough, dusty roads to the Nanyuki airstrip in Kenya. The second part of the ceremony was, therefore, postponed for two days until the morning after her anticipated return, 8 February.

The public reading of the proclamation, the traditional ceremony that takes the place of the ancient *gyratio*, followed immediately after the second meeting of the Accession Council, which was this time attended by 170 Privy Councillors. The proclamation was first read at Friary Court, St James's Palace. The Accession Council had met at ten o'clock; the proclamation was first made at St James's at eleven o'clock and at that moment flags throughout the country flew at full mast again, with the solitary exception of the Cross of St George flag which remained at half-mast over the tiny Sandringham church of St Mary Magdalene. There was snow on the grass of St James's Park that morning, but the ceremony was one of brilliant colour as the state trumpeters took their places on the balcony from which the proclamation is made. Behind them came the Garter King of Arms followed by the Heralds and Pursuivants of England, all officers of the College of Arms, wearing tabards emblazoned in brilliant gold, blue and red. There, too, making the first of his state appearances in the role of Earl Marshal of England, was the Duke of Norfolk in his full ceremonial uniform. After a fanfare of trumpets, the Garter King of Arms read the proclamation, ending with the traditional cry of 'God Save the Queen'. The trumpeters' fanfare was an overture to the National Anthem, played by the Coldstream Guards – with distant percussion effects provided by the salute of guns in Hyde Park. Then the Household Cavalry led a carriage procession first to Trafalgar Square and the statue of Charles I, from there to Temple Bar, and finally to the Royal Exchange, the proclamation being read at each place.

Simultaneously the proclamation was being read in the cities, towns and ancient boroughs throughout the country, and then throughout the Commonwealth. In Caernarvon it was read twice, in English and Welsh. In Ceylon it was read in three languages – English, Sinhalese and Tamil. Canada was 'out of step'. The Canadians did not wait for the Accession Council in London. Indeed, they did not have to, for they proclaimed Elizabeth 'Queen of Canada, and Head of the Commonwealth'. Elizabeth had

The Queen stands with the Queen Mother and Princess Margaret next to the train which was to take her father's body to its final resting place at Windsor.

God Save the Queen! The accession proclamation on the steps of the Royal Exchange. The proclamation was read out simultaneously in cities throughout the Commonwealth.

in fact become quite separately the Queen of seven nations – of the United Kingdom, of Canada, of Australia, of New Zealand, of South Africa, of Pakistan and of Ceylon.

When Edward VIII had been proclaimed, the significant face at the Palace window had been that of Mrs Wallis Simpson. The face at the window this time was that of Winston Churchill, now seventy-seven. This was the beginning of the sixth reign he had lived in. It was noted, even from a distance, that the Prime Minister's face betrayed glumness. Churchill was indeed glum. The war had brought him close to George VI, for whose personal courage he had come to have a deep admiration. It was hard for him, at his age, to reconcile himself to the idea of a young woman of twenty-five in the role of monarch. 'I don't know her,' he told his private secretary. 'She's a mere child.' But he soon got to know her, and in a very short time his weekly audiences at the Palace lengthened and lengthened. The coronation was to be sixteen months away, and soon after the proclamation he suffered an arterial spasm and temporarily lost control of his speech. It was believed by those close to him that he was deteriorating, and that what was now keeping him going was a determination to attend the crowning of the Queen.

Churchill soon realized that to stage a fairy-tale coronation of a beautiful young queen, romanticizing the event as the beginning of a new Elizabethan era, could be of incalculable value to the spirit of the people, would strengthen the position of the monarchy and be of immeasurable international consequence to the nation. The coronation would be expensive. The civil estimates for 1952 would provide £360,000; £1,200,000 would be required in 1953. Even with £648,000 recovered from the sale of seats it was still going to be a million-pound one-day pageant. On the other hand David Eccles, whom Churchill appointed as Minister of Public Buildings and Works, could justify his estimated costing as 'thrifty'. The 1952–3 election and inauguration of President Eisenhower was to cost £25 million – and no regalia!

A coronation commission was established in April and met for the first time the next month. Under the chairmanship of Prince Philip, its members included the Earl Marshal, Churchill, the Archbishop of Canterbury, Privy Councillors, members of the cabinet and Commonwealth Prime Ministers. The Earl Marshal had to mastermind the whole of the coronation arrangements; not only had he done the job before, but there was a long history of coronations and examples of the chaos that followed when things went wrong. He approached the operation with a down-to-earth attitude. 'Solve

An informal study of the Queen playing happily with her children
shortly after her accession to the throne.

the problem of what they call the toilets and you will have made a very good start indeed,' he told members of his staff at the outset. His second-in-command was the Garter King of Arms, the Hon. Sir George Rothe Bellew. Then, on the practical side, he had David Eccles, who described his own role as that of being 'The Earl Marshal's handyman'.

The Minister was to be the builder, the decorator, the electrician, the stage hand, the scene painter and the stage-door keeper for 'the greatest show on earth'. 'My job', David Eccles said at his first press conference, 'is to set the stage and to build a theatre inside Westminster Abbey. It is also to provide seats, standing room and decorations along that part of the processional route which is Crown property; to arrange flowers, floodlighting, fireworks and other expressions of public rejoicing; and to take care of newspapermen, broadcasters and cameramen.' All this was to be done under warrants of the Earl Marshal. It involved at one extreme the complete building and furnishing of an annexe at the western end of the Abbey, to be used as an assembly point for the processions and to provide retiring rooms for the Queen, the Duke of Edinburgh and other members of the royal family ... down to such details of foresight as instructing the architects designing the stands for over 100,000 people that the timber had to be cut in lengths suitable for re-use in house-building afterwards. Arrangements had to be put in hand for ten acres of flowers, grown to bloom on exactly the right day – which was to prove the coldest June day of the century.

A coronation is, literally, a ceremony of crowning, and the crown is therefore the focal point. On the day of the ceremony, the Queen was to wear Queen Victoria's diadem on her way to the Abbey. In the Abbey she would be crowned with St Edward's Crown, and throughout the procession she would wear the Imperial State Crown.

The crown has not always been an emblem of royalty. Its pagan origin is in the head wreaths of flowers made by young girls for their own adornment. From this developed the garland-crown given as a victory emblem in games. A soldier who saved a companion from death, in Roman times, was given a crown of oak leaves and acorns. The head emblem of monarchy was originally a linen or silk band worn round the forehead. This diadem eventually became more elaborate and took the form of a circlet of gold. It was during the early period of Roman imperialism that the elaborate crown made its first real appearance – but it was not worn by the emperors. The *corona muralis*, for example, was a crown of gold decorated with turrets, awarded to the soldier who was first to scale the walls of a

Self described as builder, decorator, electrician, stage hand scene painter and stage-door keeper of the coronation, David Eccles, Minister of Works, charted the progress of preparations for the event at his Lambeth Bridge headquarters.

700 miles of tubular scaffolding went into the building of stands for over 100,000 spectators on the processional routes. It was as big a painting job as painting the Forth Bridge.

besieged place. The *corona vallaris*, decorated with pales, was awarded to the soldier who first forced an entrenchment. The *corona navalis*, decorated with the shapes of ships' prows, was given for a victory at sea, and the *corona obsidionalis* was awarded to a general who had delivered a Roman army from a blockade.

Gradually the gold fillet diadem of the Roman emperors developed into a radiated crown, denoting a claim to divine honours. The earliest such 'royal' crown in existence, reputed to be over 1,500 years old, is the Iron Crown of Lombardy, preserved in the cathedral founded in 595 by Queen Theolinda at Monza, eight miles north of Milan. It is a narrow band of iron, enclosed in a circlet of six plates of gold, hinged together, jewelled and enamelled. When Napoleon was crowned King of Italy at Milan he took this crown and placed it on his own head, saying: 'God has given it to me; let him beware who would touch it.' The iron in the crown of Lombardy is reputed to have been taken from nails used in the crucifixion, and is said never to have rusted.

English crowns before the Norman conquest appear to have been fillets of pearls, the true crown being introduced by William the Conqueror – a plain gold circlet, heightened with four spikes which had trefoil heads. Henry I enriched the circlet with gems. Although it was further embellished by each successive monarch, this simple form of crown was retained until Henry IV had the first really elaborate royal crown made for his coronation. Unfortunately the Harry Crown, as it was known, did not last long. Henry V had it broken up and used as security for a loan he needed to finance his expedition to France. The arched crown, surmounted with orb and cross in its most simple form, was introduced by Henry V in preference to the crown of his predecessor. Elizabeth I introduced the velvet cap lining.

The Royal regalia and a collection of English crowns and royal diadems supposedly going as far back as King Alfred's Crown – 'gold wyerwork, set with slight stones and two little bells' – was originally kept in Westminster Abbey. On 7 March 1649, following the execution of Charles I, Parliament declared that, 'Royalty is useless, burdensome and dangerous for England.' An order was made to take possession of all the symbols of royalty kept in the Abbey – which were then broken up and defaced. Charles II's coronation in 1661 had to be delayed until new regalia was made. The crown made for him was to be worn also by James II, William III and Queen Anne. Known as St Edward's Crown, because it is so heavy (it weighs seven pounds), it was not worn at coronations after that of George III in 1761 until George V decided to revive its use. Most of the regalia still used is that which

The coronation of Henry III: the regalia and the rituals of the coronation ceremony have changed little since the Middle Ages.

A painting by Sir George Hayter of Queen Victoria's coronation. On the right, in the background can be seen the trumpets which sound the fanfare when the sovereign is crowned, and all round the Queen's peers put on their coronets as a symbol of respect to their new monarch.

was made for Charles II by the King's Goldsmith at a total cost of £31,978 9s. 11d.

The most valuable crown ever made was the one Elizabeth would wear after leaving the Abbey – the Imperial State Crown, made in 1838 for Queen Victoria. Its framework is of platinum, and the arches are set with 2,700 diamonds and hundreds of other jewels. Although the Cromwellians destroyed the regalia, many of the jewels were bought by Royalists and later came back to the Crown. Among these, and incorporated into Victoria's coronation crown, were the ruby that had belonged to the Black Prince, the sapphire that had been in the original St Edward's Crown and the four pearls that Elizabeth I had worn as ear-rings. Mounted in the front of Victoria's crown is the smaller of the two 'Star of Africa' diamonds that were cut from the Cullinan diamond, the largest diamond ever found. Although before her coronation the Queen wore only the diamond circlet – known as Queen Victoria's diadem but actually made for George IV – which is usually shown on postage stamps, the Imperial State Crown had been taken from the Tower and moved soon after her succession to the Crown Jewellers for alterations to fit the Queen's head. This crown was especially designed to be light enough for the young Queen Victoria to wear, and it was assumed that now Elizabeth would be crowned with it for the same reason. However, as the time for the coronation approached, she decided to see if she would be able to wear St Edward's Crown for the necessary period of time.

The Duke of Norfolk was so timing things down to the last second that, three months before the ceremony, he said that the actual crowning would take place 'at approximately 12.34' – and in the event the crown was placed on the Queen's head at precisely 12.33 and thirty seconds.

The Queen watched the rehearsals, familiarizing herself with all the procedure. Although she had the ballroom at Buckingham Palace marked out with posts and tapes to represent the Abbey and rehearsed privately to the timing of recordings of her father's coronation, it was felt that she should not, because of the solemnity of the event itself, take part personally in the essential Abbey rehearsals. The Duchess of Norfolk therefore stood in for her. The Queen did, however, decide that she must go through the section of the ceremony in which, if she was to be crowned with it, she would have to wear the heavy St Edward's Crown. On the strength of that rehearsal she decided that she would not only wear the St Edward's Crown for the crowning but that she would be the only modern sovereign to wear it for the rest of the ceremony instead of changing it for the lighter Imperial State

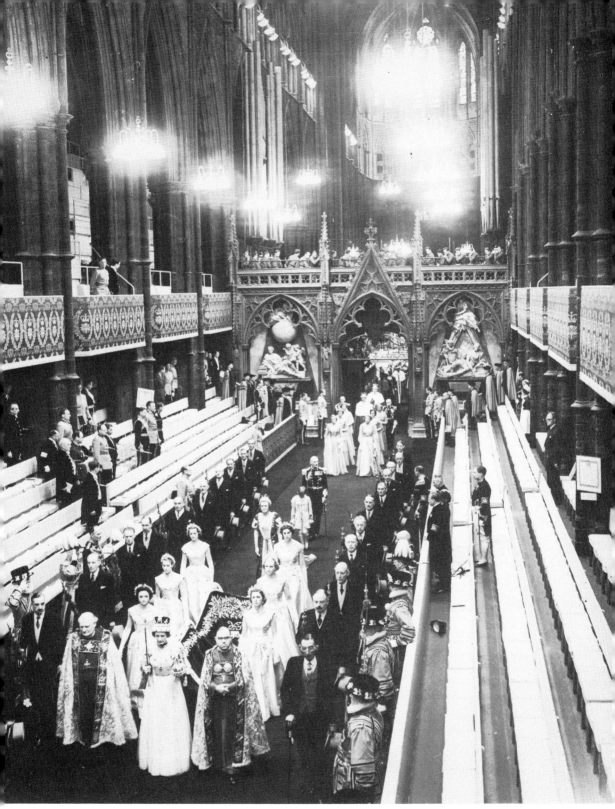

Perhaps the most extraordinary coronation picture there has ever been! The setting is Westminster Abbey. With one exception, all those taking part, although not robed for their roles, are rehearsing for the coronation of Queen Elizabeth II. The exception is the Duchess of Norfolk, who is taking the part of the Queen.

Crown, as her father had done, after the temporary removal of the crown for the communion.

Each piece of the regalia, which together form all the symbols of the monarch's secular power, has its history and tradition. Next in importance to the crown is the orb. The orb is a globe of gold, a symbol first used by Roman emperors to signify their universal dominance. It is surmounted by a cross which the Romans added after they adopted the Christian religion. The royal Orb is six and a half inches in diameter and eleven inches high. It is girdled by a band of diamonds, emeralds, rubies, sapphires and pearls while another band of jewels forms the arch above the globe. On the summit is a large amethyst. It weighs about three pounds – an unexpected and un-anticipated weight to Victoria who, on having it placed in her hand at her coronation, expressed audible surprise.

There are three sceptres. The first of these is the Sceptre with the Cross. This gold staff is about three feet long and in its head is the larger of the 'Star of Africa' diamonds – a diamond of 530 carats which can be detached to be worn as a pendant. This sceptre is given to the monarch to take in the right hand as a symbol of 'kingly power and justice'.

The second sceptre is known as the Virge and dates back to the coronation of Richard 1 in 1189. It is also known as the Sceptre with the Dove. The dove symbolizes the Holy Ghost, and this sceptre is given for the newly crowned monarch to hold in the left hand as a symbol of the sovereign's prerogative of mercy to be exercised, literally, hand in hand with justice. For this reason two sceptres are given at the same time.

The third sceptre is known as St Edward's Staff and it is reputed to contain wood taken from the cross. It is about four and a half feet in length and terminates at the top with an orb. It is carried before the sovereign in the coronation procession.

There are five swords which make a traditional appearance at the corona-tion. The first is the Sword of State, a great four-foot, two-handed sword weighing eight pounds, with the arms of William and Mary on its crimson scabbard. It is carried upright in front of the sovereign on all state occasions – quite a physical feat in 1953 for the elderly Marquess of Salisbury who had to carry it from the time the Queen entered the Abbey until after the anointing. This great sword used to be girded on to the new sovereign until after 1761, and was indeed girded on to Queen Anne at her coronation. George IV had a jewelled Sword of State designed – considered to be the most magnificent and the most valuable sword ever made. Its scabbard blazes with diamonds, emeralds and sapphires which form the Tudor rose, the thistle and the shamrock. Since George IV's coronation this sword has been girded on to kings, but Victoria decided that even this lighter sword was not a part of the regalia a woman should be required to wear and instead it was placed into her hands – a precedent to be followed by Elizabeth.

The Sword of Mercy, one of the other three swords among the coronation regalia, has a legend going far back beyond the present sword made for Charles II. The original, destroyed by the Cromwellians, was supposed to have once belonged to Ogier the Dane in about AD 760. Supposedly a voice from heaven commanded him to show mercy as he was about to strike with his sword. The sword later passed into the keeping of Edward the Confessor.

The other two ceremonial swords are the Sword of Justice to the Spirituality and the Sword of Justice to the Temporality. The first implies the sovereign's authority over the clergy, the second authority over the people.

A ring, known as 'the wedding ring of England,' is one of the oldest objects used at British coronations. It has been used to symbolize the union between the monarch and his subjects since the time of Edgar in 971. The ring Queen Elizabeth was to wear was originally made for William IV and has been used at every coronation since then except that of Victoria. It has a cross of rubies on a sapphire setting.

Gold spurs, as symbols of chivalry, have been used at coronations since the time of Richard I. Originally they were fastened to the buskins. Later they became merely touched to the heels of a king being crowned, or offered to the hand of a queen to be touched.

Until the time of the first Elizabeth, part of the ritual had been the putting on of the armillae, gold bracelets which symbolized a bond of sincerity. Forty-four years later, when the coronation of James I was being prepared, the word armillae was mistranslated to mean 'stole'. This was the origin of the Royal Stole, which had by now become a part of the ceremonial robing. The bracelets had never been used after the coronation of Elizabeth I, but research now revealed the 300-year-old mistake, and the Commonwealth nations presented new gold bracelets for the second Elizabeth, so that the ceremony could be restored.

The oldest piece of the regalia is the twin-bowl Anointing Spoon. It is supposed to be the only relic of the ancient regalia that survived the destruction of 1649.

Although the priceless regalia was not to be taken to the Abbey until just before the coronation, the question of who should carry each item on its crimson cushion in the procession from the Vestibule into the Abbey had to be judicially decided long in advance. Many of the services now claimed as great honours, often linked to an ancient family title, were in their origins very menial tasks. When they were established in feudal days they had been reminders to the king's chief tenants that, whatever their personal wealth and power, they were still his servants. Often the humble task, like that of bringing the salt to the king's table on some formal occasion, was the token payment for a great estate. A present-day 'right' to carry some part of the regalia at a coronation, or to play some other traditional role in the ritualistic ceremony, can date back to Norman times and involve the applicant in establishing a right of inheritance to be traced intricately through nearly a thousand years.

Some time in the thirteenth century the disputes about who had the traditional right to perform some particular service that had come to have the value of prestige became so contentious that a court of appeal was set up to decide between rival claimants. A court was convened by Royal Proclamation on 31 October 1952 to deal with the claims of those who: 'by ancient customs and usages, as also in regard of divers tenures of sundry manors, lands and other hereditaments, do claim and are bound to do and perform divers several services at the time of our said coronation'. The Lord Chancellor, Lord Simonds, presided over a court composed of the foremost judicial authorities, including the Lord Chief Justice of England, the Lord Justice General of Scotland and the Lord Chief Justice of Northern Ireland.

Every service and function in the ceremony has to be confirmed by this court. Even the right of the Archbishop of Canterbury has been contested in the past. And, of course, there could always be reasons why the holder of a recognizable hereditary right might be considered unsuitable by the court. For example, since the time of Richard I the Bishop of Durham and the Bishop of Bath and Wells have had the privilege of 'supporting' the sovereign throughout the coronation ceremony. It was, on some occasions, a very practical service they gave. The crown Victoria found too heavy to wear, but which Elizabeth II insisted upon using, proved too heavy and uncomfortable for some of its wearers and there were occasions when the bishops held it over the new king's head. When Richard II was crowned, the ceremony was so exhausting for the boy king that the two bishops had to hold him up for much of the time. And Queen Anne was so crippled with gout that she had to rely upon the bishops to raise her to her feet whenever she was required to stand. But the bishops had sometimes been unacceptable. Henry VII's court of claims had rejected them because of their known and contentious political sympathies. They were similarly rejected for the coronation of William and Mary in 1689.

The approved Souvenir Programme of the coronation.

Most of the claims the court had to deal with were not in dispute in 1952, but a few required counsel, legal arguments and judicial rulings. Lord Hastings and Lord Churston were rival claimants for the privilege of carrying the golden spurs. The court decided that they should carry one each. The Duke of Newcastle claimed that as Lord of the Manor of Worksop his was the right to present the embroidered glove worn on the right hand of the sovereign while holding the first of the sceptres presented to her. This claim dated back to a tradition established in 1377, when the service of the glove had gone with the ownership of the Manor of Farnham, Buckinghamshire. Farnham Manor was later exchanged between the Earl of Shrewsbury and Henry VIII for the Manor of Worksop, and the coronation 'glove service' had been legally transferred. However, in 1952 a new situation had arisen for the court of claims to deal with – the acquisition of ancient estates, and traditional rights associated with them, by investment companies. This is what had happened to the Manor of Worksop, which now, in fact, had its title registered under the name of a limited company. The court reserved judgment and later disallowed the claim and, at the coronation, the glove was presented to the Queen by Lord Woolton.

The court has the power both to change an office and even to abolish it. On this occasion the barons of the Cinque Ports made their claim to bear the traditional canopy over the Sovereign. This duty had been first given them by King John. At William IV's coronation they had been left out because the new King disapproved of the cost of great pageantry and had had only what was called at the time 'King William's penny coronation'. On this occasion, as there was already some doubt about the use of a canopy, except for the Anointing, the applicants made an alternative claim to be assigned 'stations in attendance' of the Queen. The canopy they would have carried was not in fact used, but precedent was established for the barons of the Cinque Ports – Hastings, Romney, Hythe, Dover and Sandwich – to take up station by the Abbey choir entrance and there to receive the standards from their bearers.

The most colourful of all ancient coronation offices used to be that of the King's Champion. It began at the coronation of William the Conqueror. William decided to dramatize the event by holding it on Christmas Day in the new Abbey of Westminster, the last work of Edward the Confessor. William was accompanied as he rode to the Abbey by 260 of his most stalwart chiefs, among them Robert de Marmyon. Both the Norman invaders and the conquered English had to be asked, in their own languages, to accept the new King. Robert de Marmyon created the office of King's Champion by throwing down his gauntlet and challenging to combat any man who questioned the new King's right to the throne. Unfortunately those inside the Abbey, Normans and English, acclaimed the king so boisterously that the troops outside, who were of course, Normans, believed that their compatriots in the Abbey were being attacked by the English. Immediately the Normans rushed to the houses in the neighbourhood and set them on fire. Others drew their swords and rushed into the church. And while the Normans thought that the English had staged an uprising, the English supposed they had been tricked into being victims of a massacre. The Abbey was quickly emptied of everybody but the King, the archbishop Ealdred and a few terrified priests. William refused to postpone the ceremony and it continued while fighting and plundering raged outside against a backcloth of smoke and flames. Apart from the King, the man who came out well from this coronation was Robert de Marmyon, on whom was bestowed the castle of Tamworth and the manor of Scrivelsby, together with the appointment of King's Champion.

The male line of Marmyons failed soon after the coronation of Edward III in 1327. By that time Tamworth Castle belonged to Baldwin de Freville. The manor of Scrivelsby, however, was held, because he had married a Marmyon, by Sir John Dymoke. The court of claims decided, when the Dymoke claim was disputed by Baldwin de Freville in the coronation appointments of Richard II in 1377, that the true 'King's Champion' was Sir John Dymoke. From that time, until the court of claims decided to abandon the custom on the occasion of the coronation of Edward VII, a member of the Dymoke family, in full armour, always rode into Westminster Hall during the coronation banquet to make the challenge which, for 300 years, was never taken up.

There was one slight deviation from the rule of 'inherited privilege'. At the coronation of George IV the member of the Dymoke family entitled to make the claim was a clergyman. The court of claims allowed him to perform the office by proxy. Colourful though this ceremony was, the incident of the clergyman, and an earlier episode at the coronation of Queen Anne, persuaded the court that what had been in character for William the Conqueror presented an element of risk in the twentieth century. At the coronation of George III the Champion, in heavy, cumbersome armour, had ridden into the hall on the grey charger which George II had ridden at the battle of Dettingen. His reward was a large silver bowl and cover. At earlier coronations the Champion had been awarded a gold cup for making his challenge. Sir Edward Dymoke was awarded two – one for being

Queen Mary's Champion and, hardly more than five years later, another for being Elizabeth I's Champion. For Queen Anne's coronation the Champion wore a suit of gold and silver armour, with a plume of red, white and blue feathers above his helmet. Unfortunately a fanfare of trumpets frightened his horse and as it reared up he temporarily lost control of it and there was a scene of panic. But even if customs have to change, traditions mould themselves to new circumstances, and the court of claims exists to keep them alive. Captain John L. M. Dymoke was confirmed by the 1952 court in his appointment to carry the Union Standard in the coronation procession in Westminster Abbey at the crowning of Queen Elizabeth II.

4

Preparations for a Coronation

THE THING THAT WORRIED the Duke of Norfolk was that when he had
been responsible for the coronation of George VI in 1937 he had lost a wager
he had made that he would so organize the programme of events that he
could forecast the precise time of the crowning. Every minute that his forecast
was out would cost him £1. He lost £5.

The Earl Marshal had a reputation for being rather dour. He was also
known to be an extremely competent and self-confident man, with an auth-
oritative manner. It was he who, when the operation began, said that he
believed in getting to know 'all the nuts and bolts' of the job. The 'nuts
and bolts' were things like 2,000 special chairs and 5,700 stools for the
Abbey; 3,000 square yards of chenille Axminster carpet at a cost of £18,000
from Templeton's mills in Scotland; an X-ray of the coronation chair, to
make sure that it was safe. He had to organize the safe transport, from the
Tower of London to the Goldsmiths' and Silversmiths' Company in Regent
Street, of £20,000,000 worth of diamonds, rubies, emeralds and sapphires;
and their later removal, after they had been cleaned, to the Abbey. Stands
had to be constructed for over 100,000 people, using over 700 miles of tubular scaffolding, and they had to be tested so that the historic occasion should
not be marred by what would have been a major disaster. And the 'nuts and
bolts' of *that* particular problem was getting 500 volunteer guardsmen and
Royal Artillery men to act as an 'excess weight' test crowd. Three sixty-
foot triumphal arches had to be erected in the Mall. 7,700 invitations to the
Abbey had to be printed and sent. All the problems that arose out of the
new problem of television coverage, together with the needs of 2,000 journa-
lists and 500 photographers and radio as well as TV coverage, had to be dealt
with – all the catering for a world-wide communications network embrac-
ing about a hundred nations on a scale never before known or imagined.

The one big issue during the early part of the coronation planning was that

On 31 March, 500 volunteer guardsmen and Royal Artillery men paraded outside Westminster Abbey. They were there to test the stands inside the Abbey.

Identifiable as 'the voice of British life and tradition' on the broadcasting media of radio and now also of television, Richard Dimbleby's success lay partly in the depth of research that always lay behind his quiet commentary. Here he is questioning a Tower of London Yeoman Warder.

of television. The first TV service in the world had begun in England in 1937, but there had been only 10,000 sets in use, in the London area, when the war had caused a break. In 1952 the single BBC black-and-white service was being received by one and a half million licence holders – against radio's eleven million licences for sound. The trade estimated that if the coronation were given the coverage the BBC wanted to give it, then they could sell another million and a quarter sets by 'The Day'. The BBC estimated that for such an event there would be ten viewers crowded round every set. The potential audience in Britain alone would be over twenty-seven million people – more than half the population of the country. And this vast and involved audience would see far more than anyone there, on the stands or even privileged to be in the Abbey.

The Abbey authorities were opposed to television cameras, and so was the Archbishop of Canterbury. Many politicians held similar views and even the Prime Minister, Churchill, was against the idea, because he feared that the essential dignity of the ceremony might be lost if an audience of millions was watching every moment of it. It was argued that the Queen had enough to contend with without the peep-show television cameras. It was argued that the slightest slip or mishap would be witnessed by half the nation. It was argued that the very circumstances in which many people would be watching the ceremony, at home over coffee cups, in pubs with pints of beer, was not compatible with the solemnity of the event. And it was felt that the newsreel companies, with a world audience of 350 million, with their established know-how and their ability to edit out any slip-up, would do a perfectly adequate job and that there was no need for live television coverage of the service.

On 22 October the Earl Marshal announced that:

> The Coronation Joint Executive Committee, with the consent of the Coronation Commission, and after receiving the advice of the Cabinet, has decided that still photographs, black and white films and colour films will be allowed within Westminster Abbey during the ceremony. A sound broadcast of the ceremony will also take place. Live television will be restricted to the procession west of the choir screen, but a film of the ceremony will be available for subsequent showing.

By now about two million homes had television, and every newspaper headline on 23 October summarized angry editorial protest at the ban. Eighty MPs tabled a motion against the restriction. Churchill was asked what the cabinet's advice to the Earl Marshal had been. By then the Prime Minister had realized that a hornet's nest had been aroused and he temporized – this was not a matter on which the cabinet alone advised the crown and, anyway, it was probably premature for any full statement. The coronation committee then announced that the Earl Marshal was in touch with the BBC about the situation. To provide a face-saver for everybody concerned in what was now considered an embarrassing situation, the BBC was blamed for possibly not explaining how inconspicuous the TV cameras would be, how the use of telephoto lenses would allow close-up shots to be taken discreetly and how a producer edits the programme being transmitted.

The BBC now submitted a 'shooting script' and detailed explanations of their techniques. The Queen herself broke the deadlock by inviting the Archbishop of Canterbury to a Palace luncheon with BBC executives. At this time the leading commentator was unquestionably Richard Dimbleby whose euphonious delivery had become a traditional part of great and solemn occasions. Dimbleby was asked whether he would prefer to do the radio or the television commentary from the Abbey, and which he thought to be the more important. Even before live pictures of the ceremony inside the Abbey had been agreed upon he chose, without hesitation, the television commentary job. Early in December it was announced that, with the approval of the Queen, 'parts of the service east of the screen' would be televised.

By this time the equipment for lighting the Abbey for the needs of colour newsreel films had been the subject of a great deal of experiment. The critical factor was to flood the Abbey with light not necessarily of blinding intensity but of the correct 'colour temperature' for the films being used. The main lighting equipment was mounted about sixty feet above the 'theatre' it was to illuminate, while the existing chandeliers were also used. A costumed procession of stand-ins had been filmed, and the results were completely successful. This lighting would do for the television cameras since colour television for the general British public was still a long way into the future. But while governments were to drag their feet on this issue and other countries were to steal the lead, British television was nevertheless to make history with outside-broadcast colour coverage of the coronation.

Pye of Cambridge were then leading the world in their colour television work, and they were given permission to set up three cameras and a portable transmitter on the roof of the Foreign Office. They then made arrangements to instal two twenty-inch screen receivers in the Hospital for Sick Children in Great Ormond Street where, with what proved to be a completely successful experiment, 150 children were to be the first colour TV viewers in Britain.

In New York, the coronation day broadcast began at 2.45 am. Bars in the city stayed open and all-night customers listened to the live sound broadcast while they watched prepared film material on the small TV screens of the time.

Although not yet a nationwide service, the BBC's single channel, 405 line black and white television service gave an estimated 27 million viewers full coverage of the processions and of the Abbey ceremony – among that vast new audience, these patients and staff at St George's Hospital, Hyde Park Corner.

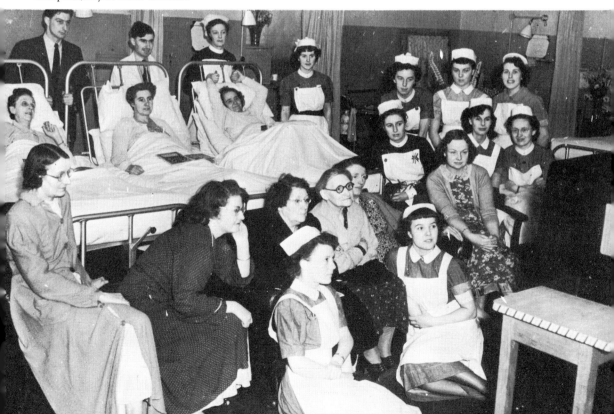

The BBC's more comprehensive black-and-white coverage was to be relayed to stations in France, West Germany and Holland, requiring separate language commentaries and involving technical problems of translating the signal into the different line standard used at that time on the continent. The biggest problem that faced the engineers was to span, without booster stations, 100 miles of Russian Zone to get the picture to Berlin. It was hoped to extend the European link-up so that the coronation could be watched in places like Berlin, Hamburg and Bad Oeynhausen where the British Army of the Rhine had their headquarters. British servicemen and their wives in Germany were, in the event, to watch the coronation in thirty-four NAAFI clubs between Cologne and Berlin. And in Paris, visitors at the home of an American society hostess because they did not have a set of their own, the Duke and Duchess of Windsor – once better known as Edward VIII and Wallis Simpson – were to be viewers.

The planning for the nation-wide and world-wide communications on coronation day built up into such a pattern of complexity and efficiency that the American network men, who supposed that they knew it all, were left open-mouthed. More than a hundred international commentators, speaking in forty-two different languages, were able to go on the air simultaneously. To feed five main radio networks BBC engineers had to site and erect over eighty control points. There were 1,300 additional sound circuits, and over a hundred vision circuits connecting the control positions with their different networks. Television alone was to supply seven hours of vision on the coronation and to record 60,000 feet of film. Every line and every panel in the control points was duplicated in case of failure. Every commentator was supplied with a spare microphone. In case of power failure a secondary battery storage system was available. The American TV networks had their own camera positions at vantage points at the Palace, along the route and outside the Abbey and arrangements were made for them to telerecord the BBC's coverage inside the Abbey.

Their problem was to get the pictures to America quickly and it was solved by fitting out aircraft as film processing and editing laboratories. Both the American networks, Columbia and the National Broadcasting Company, and the Canadian Broadcasting Company entered into what was a race. Motorcycle messengers would race film from ciné camera positions to Heathrow where the BBC TV signal would be picked up in a control room in which, by new techniques, telerecordings would be available almost instantaneously. The Canadians had borrowed three record-breaking Canberra PR3s from the RAF and equipped them for this special purpose. The Canberras would take the pictures as far as Goose Bay, Labrador. There Mustang P51s would take one set of the film and telerecordings to Boston for Columbia Broadcasting's showing on their USA network, while Canadian CF100s would fly a duplicate set to Quebec for Canadian viewers. NBC were later to organize a Canberra of their own, which would fly to Gander, refuel there, and go on direct to Boston. In the event the NBC plane ran into mechanical trouble when it was two hours out across the Atlantic, and it had to turn back. In view of this apparently disastrous setback, the network fell back on earlier plans to take the BBC material from the RAF planes at Goose Bay. And although their own procession material failed to be available they managed to get on to the air a few minutes before NBC. That evening 85,000,000 Americans were to watch the coronation on TV.

The arrangements for newspaper coverage, although complex, were of course familiar. Even so the GPO engineers had to put in 3,280 special telephone circuits and to provide direct lines from stands, rooftops and the Abbey for use by the biggest international assembly of reporters and commentators ever gathered together for a single event.

'To build a theatre inside Westminster Abbey', had been David Eccles' description of part of the work delegated by the Earl Marshal's warrant. Originally, and in the days when the King's Champion's role was as valid to the ceremony as the TV commentator's voice was in 1953, the Westminster Abbey ceremony had been almost an incidental part of the background of a coronation. The real coronation, from Norman times until the coronation of William IV in 1831, had taken place at the coronation banquet. This had been given in the Great Hall in the Palace of Westminster, and it was here that the king had been enthroned. Westminster Hall is all that remains, today, of the old Palace. Some coronation celebrations had gone on for two days. It had been during these celebrations that the clergy had come over in a procession, carrying the religious regalia, to invite the king and his peers to come to the Abbey for a service of consecration.

The banquet ceremony was abandoned for Victoria's coronation, since it had become the subject of public criticism as an excuse for dissipation, intemperance and general excesses. For that coronation, however, a great gallery of tiered seats had been built inside the Abbey, and this had been the cause of damage to some of the royal tombs. The problem was that the service of consecration, originally the only part of the coronation ceremony that took place in the Abbey, had not been intended to be a spectacle witnessed by 7,700 people. When William the Conqueror had been crowned there, the Abbey had been 'St Edward's Church', begun by Edward the Confessor in 1065. Henry III, in the opening phase of the great age of English Gothic architecture – but influenced by contemporary French architecture – almost completely demolished St Edward's Church, of which only a little now remains in the pyx-house and the south side of the cloisters. But although the new Abbey was built by Henry to be a burial place for kings, and the coronation church for their successors, Henry had not envisaged more than a few hundred noblemen and religious leaders ever witnessing the ceremony.

The congregation in the nave can see only the procession. Only the witnesses in the first twelve rows of the transepts have a view of 'the place of crowning'. In 1953 the television audience of millions were to have a far better as well as a much more complete view of the Abbey procession and ceremony than anyone who was present.

The preparations in the Abbey began on 1 December, 1952, when the nave was closed to the public. A month later David Eccles' Ministry took over the entire building. The work that lay ahead involved building staircases to the galleries high up in the towering structure of the Abbey. A telephone exchange, camera positions, lavatories, sleeping quarters for soldiers, police and security staff, and five medical centres to be staffed by twenty-five doctors, thirty nurses and twenty stretcher-bearers – these were among the basic requirements for the event. Miles of cables for telephones, for lighting, and the TV and radio lines had to be laid and concealed. Control rooms for lighting, for the public address system and for security control were all needed. Air conditioning had to be built in. A new floor had to be laid – sand and felting levelling off the existing floor before the new timber floor was put down. A raised platform, stretching from in front of the high altar almost to the choir, was to be built for the ceremony to be performed upon it – and records showed that just such a platform had been built for the coronation of Elizabeth I. A temporary trolley railway was installed to carry heavy building materials from the west door to the broad sanctuary. In Elizabeth I's time, the records showed, they had used sledges for this purpose, with a heavy timber 'track'. There would be, altogether, 500 participants in the actual ceremony.

It needs to be explained that these were days of shortages and of profiteering. Timber and building materials were in short supply. Builders to construct urgently needed homes, and to repair war damage, were in great demand. David Eccles had to justify the work at the Abbey to critics in the House of Commons. By February a labour force of two hundred was engaged in

The Queen's Beasts –
inspired by Henry VIII's
Kynge's Beastes of
Hampton Court, were
placed in position outside
the temporary Annexe of
the Abbey on 29 May on
'coronation weekend'.

With ritual dictating
almost every detail, the one
thing upon which the
Queen had complete
personal choice and
decision was her
coronation gown.
Norman Hartnell
designed it. It was her
decision to incorporate the
embroidered emblems of
all the Commonwealth
countries with those of the
United Kingdom into the
fabric of the dress.

the Abbey, but he was able to say that none had been diverted from housing work. On the other hand eighty-five per cent of the timber being used in the Abbey would later be used for house building ... and the programme was 300,000 houses at this time.

A large part of the workforce was engaged upon the Annexe. This was the sixth coronation for which an Annexe had been built. From the first one in 1831 for William IV until 1953, the architects of these remarkable temporary structures had gone to extravagant lengths to harmonize with the Abbey and the two dominant western towers added by Christopher Wren, under which the Annexe was always built.

The Annexe for the 1953 coronation was regarded, however, as being a little breathtaking in its departure from tradition. Apart from the Festival of Britain buildings on the South Bank site, no new post-war architectural style had yet emerged. Now there was suddenly an example for the future in an Annexe that, with boldness and imagination, showed how a modern steel framework building using clean lines could co-exist and harmonize with the Gothic architecture that told much of London's history. The western wall of the vestibule, where the processions would be assembled before they moved off into the Abbey, was designed as one enormous mullioned window, glazed in panels decorated with modern designs of the national emblems. This glazing, and the hide-covered main entrance doors under a water-lily-shaped canopy breaking an almost severe north wall, were left until just before coronation day. The really dramatic feature of the Annexe, however, was not seen until two days before the ceremony – this was the line of the Queen's Beasts, ten six-foot-high heraldic statues which were mounted, like fantasy creatures out of some splendid extravaganza, beneath the mullioned window-wall.

At his press conference to introduce the Queen's Beasts, David Eccles said of them: 'You will not meet these animals anywhere on the level of humdrum reality. But then, on that plane, there is no place for the Queen's Golden Coach. These are dream creatures, aristocrats of an heroic species, real and formidable in the world of the imagination.' The inspiration for the Queen's Beasts came from Hampton Court, where Eccles had been impressed by the sculpted, shield-carrying heraldic beasts of Henry VIII. David Eccles and Eric Bedford, the chief architect, had already agreed that the great mullioned west wall of the Annexe needed something more. Between them they now came up with the idea of adopting the Hampton Court heraldic sculptures. These originals were, of course, quite incompatible with the post-war twentieth-century design of the Annexe. Both the

Pageants like this one were staged all over Britain in coronation year. Here, finishing touches are made to a costume while two actors learn their lines in the background.

The meat ration was two shillings' worth a head per week, but eighty-two licences to roast the traditional coronation ox had been granted by the Ministry of Food. Here, children of the village of Ide Hill, near Sevenoaks, bring wood for the fire. Roasting started early on coronation day morning and the first slice was cut at 6.30 that evening.

heraldic beasts themselves, and the emblems on the shields they supported were specific to the House of Tudor. But in the Queen's wider royal ancestry there were other heraldic beasts to choose from – a total of thirty in all, though only ten were needed. A commission was given to the sculptor James Woodford to execute the work. The beasts chosen were the lion of England, the white greyhound of Richmond, the yale of Beaufort, the red dragon of Wales, the white horse of Hanover, the white lion of Mortimer, the unicorn of Scotland, the griffin of Edward III, the black bull of Clarence and the falcon of the Plantagenets.

James Woodford's Queen's Beasts were a splendid creation, unfortunately only in plaster for a very temporary purpose. But, with their shields emblazoned with the golds and scarlets and blues of heraldic colours, to many of the millions who came to London for the coronation they were the most exciting contribution to the backcloth to the event.

The last piece of the jigsaw backcloth to be fitted into place could not be constructed until the night before the coronation, but it had to be planned, and its assembly rehearsed elsewhere, at the same time as the rest of the work. This was a bridge to span St Margaret's Street and to link the Abbey to the Palace of Westminster. Its purpose in 1953 was to give an entrance to the Abbey for peers and politicians and to reduce the use of the entrance to the Abbey. The first time such a link had been used was in 1066.

On the night of 10 May 1941 incendiary bombs had showered the south-west tower. The Chapter roof went up in flames and there was scattered destruction all round the area. Among the damage it was later discovered that a phial, stored at the Deanery, had shattered. That phial had contained the supply of oil used to anoint the sovereign.

The anointing is the mystical part of the coronation ceremony, and it is this that gives the monarch spiritual sovereignty. All the regalia and the royal robes are put aside for the religious ritual, which was to be one of the only two parts of the service not shown on television.

The kings of the Bible had been anointed – Saul, David, Solomon and Jehu are among those to whose anointing there are recorded references. The ritual has always had the deepest significance in the coronations of English monarchs.

> Not all the water in the rude, rough sea
> Can wash the balm from an anointed King.

So had said Shakespeare's Richard II, giving expression to the popularly held belief that once the monarch had been anointed his sovereignty became a holy office, indissoluble. There is a legend that in 1166, when he was living in Sens in exile, Thomas à Becket was visited by a vision of the Virgin. Becket had fled to France to escape the anger of Henry II, and was under the protection of Pope Alexander and King Louis. The Virgin gave him a phial of holy oil, saying that it was for the anointing of the kings of England – commencing, of course, with the successor to Henry, who the Virgin said was unworthy. Whether Thomas had had in mind the overthrowing of Henry, and was justifying this by claiming that the King's anointing by the previous Archbishop of Canterbury, Theobald, had not been with a true holy oil, has to be speculation. He supposedly hid the oil in the Abbey at Poitiers, in Burgundy, which was assigned to him as an asylum by the Pope. Long after Becket's murder, according to this legend, a priest from Poitiers gave the phial to the Duke of Lancaster who in turn gave it to the Black Prince.

When, in 1399, Richard II was imprisoned in the Tower, and compelled by Parliament to resign his crown, the power of Parliament both to elect Henry of Lancaster, although he was not next in line of succession, and to settle the succession on his heirs, was solemnly defined by Bishop Arundel and Thomas, Duke of Gloucester. And Henry, already foreseeing the revolt and attempted restoration of Richard only a few months later, carefully gave himself what was the better claim to sovereignty than a doubtful hereditary right – he was anointed with the holy oil from Poitiers.

The supply of this oil lasted for eleven coronations but became exhausted at the coronation of James I in 1603. It had also become stale and evil smelling, and Elizabeth I had complained about its odour, saying it was, 'a nasty grease and smelt ill'. A new oil had to be prepared for Charles I, and the apothecary kept Elizabeth's complaint and Charles I's fastidiousness in mind. An oil was made up using orange flowers, rose petals, cinnamon, jasmine, sesame, musk, civet and ambergris.

The actual amount of oil used in the coronation ceremony is very small, and so it became the custom to make a small supply which could be used for a sequence of coronations. A further supply was made for the coronation of James II in 1685, and the apothecary so pleased the new King with its perfume that he was rewarded by the then small fortune of £200.

A supply was made anew for Queen Victoria, but she reigned for so long that when it was required for the next coronation it was found to have crystallized. The firm of London pharmacists who had made the oil for Victoria made another supply which lasted for the coronations of Edward VII and George V. In 1936 they made a new supply for the coronation of Edward VIII but he, like Edward V in 1483, was never crowned or anointed and the oil was used instead for George VI. It was this phial of oil that was broken in the blitz.

There was consternation when the Earl Marshal's office tried to contact the pharmacists who made the oil. They had gone out of business. Eventually an elderly lady, who was related to members of what had been a family business, was traced and found to have kept, as a matter of interest, a few ounces of the base of the compound. The ingredients of the formula used for Charles I were known, and with the supply of base material and this formula a Bond Street chemist went to work – although before doing so he gave up smoking for four weeks to ensure that his sense of smell would be acute and reliable.

The celebrated designer Norman Hartnell was commissioned in October 1952 to design the Queen's coronation dress, and three seamstresses and six embroideresses were also engaged. The most recent precedent was the gown worn by Queen Victoria. But on 28 June 1838, more than a century before, Victoria had been an unmarried girl of eighteen, and her dress had been simple. Norman Hartnell was told that while the dress must have no exaggerated shape because of the various robes with which it would be worn, something much more regal than Victoria's dress was required.

In the *Liber Regalis*, compiled by the Abbot of Westminster in the fourteenth century, all the rituals and procedures for an English coronation were laid down. Details of the ceremonial royal vestures, similar to those worn about AD 400 by the emperors of Byzantium at their coronations in Constantinople, are given precisely in this compilation and allow no concessions to personal taste. But the gown in which she would be seen by the crowds, and would wear under the robes of investment, was, however, very much a matter in which Elizabeth could make her own decision.

She asked for white satin, and a gown along similar lines to the wedding dress Norman Hartnell had previously designed for her. Altogether he submitted nine alternative designs with floral designs to display the rose, the thistle, the shamrock and the leek. The Queen decided, however, that she would not wear the emblems of the United Kingdom without those of the Commonwealth countries. So the design was altered to incorporate such lesser-known emblems as the lotus of Ceylon, the protea of South Africa, the wattle of Australia, the wheat and jute of Pakistan, the maple leaf of Canada and the fern of New Zealand. The dress was to be covered with thousands of tiny seed pearls, each set in a small saucer of silver, so that with every movement the fabric, although it flowed freely, would seem to be

Against the backcloth of history, with the Crown, the Orb and the Sceptre and wearing the Robe of Monarchy, this was to be the official coronation picture of Queen Elizabeth II, taken by Cecil Beaton.

made of glass. The emblems – those of England, Scotland, Ireland and Wales in panels on the skirt, and the others massed deeply round the hem – were to be embroidered in full colour. Norman Hartnell also designed the complementary dresses to be worn by Princess Margaret, the Queen Mother, the Duchess of Kent, the seventeen-year-old Princess Alexandra and the six maids of honour.

For her entrance into the Abbey the Queen would wear the Royal Robe of crimson velvet, hemmed with ermine and bordered with gold lace, its heavy train carried by the maids of honour. With this she would also wear the collar of the Garter, and her diamond diadem. When the time came for the anointing she would take off her diadem and give it to the Mistress of the Robes. Then the Lord Great Chamberlain, the Marquess of Cholmondeley, would formally remove the crimson Royal Robe from her shoulders and the six maids of honour would fold it and give it to the Groom of the Robes. Finally the collar of the Garter would be removed and the Groom would carry these symbols of royalty away to St Edward's Chapel. The splendid coronation gown would then be covered by a plain white garment, put on like a coat but fastened at the back, in which she would be anointed. After the anointing the formal vesting would begin with the unfamiliar robes from the past which are worn only this once by the sovereign during the reign. Until 1953 they had only been seen by those people in the Abbey close enough personally to witness the ceremonial involving them. At this coronation, they would be seen by millions.

The first robe is known as the Colobium Sidonis. It is of white linen and opens at the side. The emperors of Byzantium had worn the *colobium sidonis*, a tunic, at their coronations. So had Edward the Confessor, who had actually been buried in his coronation robes. From the time of the coronation of Richard I in 1189, soon after Edward's tomb had been opened and the robes taken from it, it is said that these original vestments were used for every subsequent coronation until that of Charles I. The robes, then in a state of approaching disintegration anyway, were destroyed by the Cromwellians when they broke up the regalia.

The second robe is the Supertunica – a long coat of gold, lined with rose-coloured silk, and having wide, flowing arms. This is girdled at the waist by a sword belt presented by the Girdlers' Company, one of the ancient City livery companies.

Finally there is the Pallium, a Royal Robe of cloth of gold. Although the mantle worn by the Queen would have the emblems of the Commonwealth worked into its design, its four corners would show imperial eagles – as

Wearing the golden Supertunica, the Queen carries the Great Sword of State, representing justice, to the altar.

had the investment robes of the Byzantine Empire, signifying sovereignty over the four corners of the world.

Some of the fine, embroidered cloth needed for coronation costumes, robes and uniforms was made in Germany. The silk for the purple Royal Robe of State with which the Queen would be finally invested in St Edward's Chapel at the end of the ceremony, and which she would wear, in place of the crimson robe, on her return to Buckingham Palace, was spun by silkworms – as had been that for her wedding dress – at Lady Hart Dyke's silkworm farm. It was made into yarn at silk mills at Glemsford in Suffolk, dyed in Staffordshire, and woven on a handloom at the Braintree Mills in Essex. Messrs Ede and Ravenscroft in Chancery Lane, who specialize in academic, legal and royal robes, made up the material. Finally, the embroidery was carried out by the Royal School of Needlework. And while Norman Hartnell was grappling with his problems, and Ede and Ravenscroft were taking theirs in their stride because it was work they had been doing since the time of Charles II, Moss Bros, famous for their hiring facilities, were refurbishing and repairing *their* stock of robes for peers who did not possess their own.

The allocation of seats for peers and peeresses in the Abbey was, of course, limited. A ballot was made to allocate the available accommodation. Many of the unlucky peers who had their own robes immediately lent these to other peers who had been luckier in the ballot, but who did not have their own robes. Later a number of peers who had been allocated places in the Abbey found themselves less lucky in their attempts to hire or borrow robes. The official reason for absence at such an event as a coronation is usually illness, and is therefore notified only a day or two before the event. At this last minute there were enough peers who found themselves unable to attend that it was possible for the Earl Marshal's office to offer places to every peer who wanted to be there ... including those who had, of course, already lent their robes to someone else!

In addition to the royal robes a large quantity of special gold fabrics, satins, silks and damasks was needed for hangings in the Abbey, for the copes of the canons which are traditionally presented to them by a new sovereign, for the cushions and stools used by the Queen, and for relining the State Coach.

In the Royal Mews an early survey was taken of the carriages. The most important of these was, of course, the golden State Coach, designed by Sir William Chambers who was Comptroller of His Majesty's Works to George

In coronation year there was naturally a great demand for robes and uniforms which meant a lot of skilled and often last-minute work. Here, a craftsman hammers a design on to a helmet.

Putting the finishing touches to peers' coronets.

III. Chambers was responsible for Somerset House, and was considered the greatest architect of his day. The coach was built at a cost of £8000, an incredible sum in 1761, but in fact this was taxed and the King actually paid only £500. Chambers employed an Italian painter and engraver, Giambattista Cipriani, who had come to live in London, and who was one of the first Fellows of the Royal Academy, to paint the panels on the side of the coach. It is Cipriani and not Chambers who is now remembered in connection with the coach.

At the time when it was built it was criticized both for its cost and its fanciful design. Horace Walpole said: 'It is a beautiful object – though crowded with improprieties. Its palm trees denote the architect's predilection for oriental subjects. The supports are Tritons and not very well adapted for a land carriage.' But the State Coach has never been neglected during any reign. George IV had the roof raised so that he could sit upright when wearing his new, tall crown. Queen Victoria spent nearly £1000 on a hammercloth – a canopy to give shelter and cover to the driver. Edward VII not only had the hammercloth removed but he did away with the driver's box seat so that the public should have a better view of their King and Queen. This made the coachman redundant, and from then onwards each of the four pairs of horses had to be ridden by postillions.

Originally the horses used were creams, then a team of blacks was used, and later a team of bays. The Windsor Greys were used by George VI and were to be used again by Elizabeth. Their state harness was a gift from the Queen of the Netherlands in 1946. The coach, which weighs four tons, needed not only relining and regilding, but the wheels had to be reset and the Cipriani panels, which were showing signs of cracking, had to be expertly restored. The real problem for the Royal Mews, however, was that they did not have enough coaches and carriages available to accommodate all the visiting royalty and heads of state who were expected to attend.

The date of the coronation had been pushed forward into June of the year after the Queen's accession for several reasons. Time was needed for all the planning and preparations, especially as this was still a period of shortages after the war. The Queen herself was anxious that there should be long hours of daylight, and the best chance of good weather for the crowds who would undoubtedly spend many hours lining the streets and many of whom would make it an all-night wait. Finally it was necessary to give important invited guests from overseas enough time.

Seven extra carriages were borrowed from a film company and a number of coachmen were recruited privately to supplement the regular Palace

Yeomen of the Guard, arriving by coach at the Abbey for the coronation rehearsal of 29 May, prepare to go on parade.

A corporal in the Household Cavalry, who provided the Queen's escort in the procession, receives his kit.

coachmen. They had a problem ahead of them, too – they were warned that, for the first time, the seven-mile procession route would not be sanded. Officially the reason given was that, unless it was frosty, sanding was not necessary. Unofficially the reason was that sand was needed for build-ing and was in short supply, as was the extra labour that would be required. In the event sand was used – and was washed away by the rain!

A completely different aspect of preparation concerned Sir Adrian Boult, who was to conduct the music in the Abbey, and Dr William McKie who would conduct the choristers. The choir, orchestra, organists and trumpeters totalled nearly 500 people, many of whom could not see the conductor. Sir Adrian had an orchestra of sixty, drawn from the leading orchestras in the country, and under the leadership of Paul Beard. Dr McKie had a choir of more than 400, drawn from the choirs of the Abbey itself, the Chapel Royal, St Paul's Cathedral, St George's Chapel, Windsor, and other choirs repre-senting different parts of the kingdom. Part of the choir had to be accommo-dated above the nave and behind the organ. Dr McKie had to have two assistants to relay the beat his baton was signalling. But it was not a new prob-lem. On one previous occasion a conductor had semaphored instructions to the choristers.

While tradition rules the form of a coronation service, the robes and the regalia, the music has changed, and it is customary for new works and new arrangements of older works to be composed and arranged. William Walton wrote a new march, Sir Arthur Bliss a processional, and Sir Arnold Bax a coronation march for the end of the service. A Canadian, Healy Willan, composed a new anthem. Some of the traditionally used anthems were given new music, and a new setting was written for the national anthem. Rehears-ing at the Abbey was difficult for both musicians and choristers because of the builders. The coronation was hardly more than a week away before the first collective, full rehearsal of the music became possible on Sunday 24 May.

In 1296 Edward III had marched into Scotland to put down a revolt on the part of his vassal king of Scotland, John de Balliol, who had been crowned at Scone a few days after Edward had given him the throne on condition that he swore fealty. Edward swept through Scotland, capturing every stronghold within two months. On his return south from Elgin he took the famous Lia-Fail stone on which John de Balliol had been crowned in Scone Abbey. He ordered it to be removed to Westminster, to be a testi-

PREVIOUS PAGE At a cost of £10,000, the 200-year-old coronation coach had been renovated. On 22 February, more than three months before the coronation, the Queen was driven twice round the Royal Mews to test the rubber cushioning of the old iron-bound wheels. Here, she is inspecting the Windsor Greys.

The four pairs of Windsor Greys, who were to pull the State Coach on Coronation Day, out on a pacing test near Buckingham Palace. The Windsor Greys were first used by George VI.

Did Jacob's head lie on this stone, his pillow on the night of his dream of a ladder reaching to heaven? This is one of many legends about the Stone of Scone which is contained in the base of King Edward's Chair.

mony to the conquest and surrender of Scotland and to be a guarantee that no other king of Scotland could ever be crowned upon it.

The Lia-Fail, which came to be known as the Stone of Scone after its removal from Scotland, no more belonged to the Scots than it now did to the English. The legendary history of this relic, which has more mystical importance than the chair which surmounts it in Westminster Abbey, is that it is the 'stone of Beth-el'. This was the stone on which Jacob's head was resting when he had his dream vision of the ladder reaching to heaven; the Book of Genesis says: 'And Jacob rose up early in the morning, and took the stone he had put for his pillows, and poured oil upon the top of it.'

The Beth-el Stone was later taken to Spain where it was used as a Seat of Justice by Gethalus. Mysteriously the holy relic then found its way to Ireland, where it was used for the enthronement of the Irish kings of Tara, who named it the Lia-Fail. At this time it was said that when a claimant to the throne sat upon it, it gave a 'shouting noise that was heard from sea to sea' if the claim was truly founded. The Irish tribe of the Dalriads, who came from north of Antrim, migrated to Argyll in Scotland in the beginning of the sixth century. Their leader was Fergus, son of the Irish King Eric. His father gave him the Lia-Fail to take with him and to use to make himself king of the new territory. The Lia-Fail was taken to Dunstaffnage, whose castle is reputed to have been the seat of one of the first Scottish princes. Now known as the Palladium, or the Stone Chair, it was used as a coronation seat at Dunstaffnage until, in 971, Kenneth II of Scotland moved it to Scone.

By now it had acquired the mystique which made its removal to London by Edward so significant. A distich of the period summed up the new prophecy:

> Ni fallat fatum, Scoti, quocunque locatum,
> Inventient lapidem, regnare tenentur ibidem.

> Unless old prophecies are weird and vain,
> Where'er this stone is found, the Scots shall reign.

The custom of inaugurating a ruler by placing him upon a sacred stone was widespread in ancient times and the possibility must not be ruled out that the Stone of Scone only dates back to about AD 971 and that the 'Jacob's pillow' legend was attached to it to provide the necessary mystique. The fact is that the Stone is of a reddish grey sandstone which is found in the neighbourhood of Scone.

The magnificent golden State Coach: the roof is supported by stylized palm trees and a Triton stands at each corner. Built for George III, it needed highly-skilled refurbishing for Queen Elizabeth's coronation. It was relined and regilded, and the beautiful Cipriani panels on its sides had to be painstakingly restored.

Some of the Crown Jewels. Much of the regalia used in the coronation ceremony was originally made for Charles II. In the centre is the magnificent St Edward's Crown, used for the actual crowning, and in front of it are the Sword of State, which is carried in front of the sovereign on all State occasions, the Sceptre with the Dove, symbolizing mercy, and the Royal Sceptre. On the right are the two Armillae symbolizing a bond of sincerity, in the centre the eagle-shaped Ampulla containing the holy oil and the twin-bowl anointing spoon, and on the left the beautiful 'wedding ring of England'.

The Queen's coach leaves Buckingham Palace.

Sir Winston Churchill, one of the Queen's greatest admirers in spite of his initial
reservations about her youth, in the procession.

RIGHT The coronation procession
passes under Admiralty Arch,
magnificently decorated for the
occasion.

Queen Elizabeth the Queen Mother driving to the Abbey in the Irish State Coach. She was accompanied by her other daughter, Princess Margaret.

Wearing the ring and holding the two sceptres, the Queen is crowned with the St Edward's Crown. In time-honoured tradition, peers and peeresses in the congregation put on their coronets simultaneously, and the shout 'God Save the Queen' rang out.

Holding the orb and wearing the Imperial State Crown, the radiant Queen smiles happily on her way back to the Palace.

The Queen and Prince Philip, relaxed and happy after the ordeal of the coronation ceremony, wave to the demanding and jubilant crowds from the balcony of Buckingham Palace. With them are Prince Charles, Princess Anne and the Queen Mother.

And, of course, England itself had had an earlier Coronation Stone – the one which is displayed in the open at Kingston-upon-Thames. At least five and possibly seven Saxon Kings were crowned at 'Cingestune', the last of them being the nine-year-old boy King, Ethelred, whose coronation took place at the Easter Festival in 979. The first reputed use of this coronation stone was in 901, seventy years before the first authenticated use of the Stone of Scone.

The Stone has only left the Abbey twice since 1296. Cromwell had the chair moved to Westminster Hall for his own installation as Lord Protector, and during the Second World War it was taken for safe keeping to Gloucester Cathedral. The Stone was not moved, however, until Christmas Day 1950, when an adventurous group of young Scots stole it from Westminster Abbey and deposited it in Arbroath Abbey.

The great carved wooden chair that Edward III had made to fit over the Stone has been used at coronations ever since and, despite considerable abuse, is in sound condition after nearly 700 years. In the past it was covered with splendid cloth for each coronation, but the upholstery was nailed on and afterwards torn off by vandal souvenir collectors. Other visitors – and in Cromwellian times this happened in many churches throughout the country – carved their initials in the woodwork.

The real history of the Coronation Chair, and the many successive changes to it, had never been known until it was examined by modern scientific methods to make sure that it was in a safe condition for the 1953 coronation. Then a strange and romantic history was built up.

Long ago, when it had been made at Edward III's order, not for his coronation, but to contain the Stone of Destiny which was to ensure that all his successors held Scotland, it had been magnificently painted and decorated with shields and inscriptions. At some later date another artist had overpainted the original decoration with fanciful coronation scenes and symbolism. Later still, perhaps when time had dulled this unknown artist's work, the chair had been stained and varnished. There was evidence, too, of various structural changes, of the addition of the lion-supported base, and of the cutting off of carved pinnacles that had once been on the arms. For the 1953 coronation the existing arm coverings were removed and not replaced, and a new cushion of crimson damask was used.

The very considerable job of carpeting the Abbey was carried out at the beginning of May, and from then on there were rehearsals of one kind or another almost daily. The Annexe carpet could not, of course, be laid until the glazing of the mullioned West Wall was completed.

CORONATION

It was not until the night of 31 May that the Coronation Chair was put into position; then four men slid underneath it the legendary Beth-el Stone. Only when the Stone of Destiny was back in position were the Abbey preparations for the coronation considered to be complete.

5

Overture

ON WEDNESDAY 27 MAY 1953, cheering thousands, drenched in heavy rain, greeted the Queen as she drove through the decorated streets from Buckingham Palace to Westminster Hall and back. This was the overture to the coronation. The Queen was going to Westminster to welcome her prime ministers and other parliamentary representatives from the Commonwealth.

London was magnificent. The great arches in the Mall had been lifted into position by cranes. Regent Street was a great, curving bower of blossoming pink roses. Bond Street was an avenue of golden trumpets. Victoria Street offered a perspective of gold and scarlet banners. The nightingales – even if they *were* tape recorders up in the trees – sang in Berkeley Square. The statue of Eros was enclosed in a splendidly gilded cage. Selfridge's had excelled themselves with a magnificent life-size, realistic equestrian statue of the Queen, behind which was a panel painting of Elizabeth I. On each side of the display were the promises the two Elizabeths had made upon their accessions. The first Elizabeth had said: 'This kingdom hath had many wise, noble and victorious princes – but in love, care, sincerity and justice, I will compare with any prince that ever you had or shall have.' The twentieth-century Elizabeth had said: 'With a new faith in the old and splendid beliefs given us by our forefathers, and the strength to venture beyond the safeties of the past, I know we shall be worthy of our duty.'

On Thursday 28 May news editors in Fleet Street and throughout the provinces suddenly and intuitively pushed everything off the front page that was unconnected with the coronation. Thus, on that day, the highly sensational case which opened in Blackpool, in which Mrs Louisa Merrifield and her third husband, Alfred Edward, were accused of poisoning seventy-nine-year-old Mrs Sarah Ann Ricketts, to whom they acted as housekeepers, was pushed off the front page.

Only in retrospect was the *Daily Mirror*'s front page of the next day to

The face of London was greatly changed in coronation year. Decorations went up everywhere, but here, large crush barriers have been erected to prevent any accidents among the vast crowds which flocked to London to watch the celebrations.

Television was stealing its thunder, but Fleet Street, the traditional processional-route link between the cities of London and Westminster, could still put on a show in the year when most cars were still pre-war and carried EX and FX prefix characters.

have its strange and sensational news value. Of all the great and famous streets in London, one alone compelled the *Mirror*'s headline criticism: 'THE SHAME OF PICCADILLY'. It gave its front page over completely to this story, which opened:

This is the shame of Britain's most famous street, Piccadilly.

In the centre of Coronation London, Piccadilly has failed to capture the spirit of the Golden Days.

Even in back streets, where money is counted in pennies – streets not within a Coronation's roar of the great procession – pictures of the Queen are in almost every window; there are brilliant flags, golden crowns and brand new decorations.

The *Mirror* published a picture of Piccadilly, taken on 28 May. By contrast they published another picture, and a story, of a London back street. The photographer and reporter had been sent out to cover the story of one such of thousands in London. The street they picked was a cul-de-sac where the average house rent was then £1 a week, and the average wage was £8 a week. There were forty houses in the street. The street's coronation committee had raised nearly £115. The decorations – 750 flags, a banner proclaiming 'Long Live The Queen', and floodlighting – were 'smashing', the *Mirror* reported.

The paper named the street, but it is no longer to be found in London gazetteers, for Rillington Place, in Notting Hill, later changed the name that was soon to become notorious as the background to the most horrific series of murders in London since the days of Jack the Ripper – the murders committed by John Christie.

The invasion of London had begun on 23 May, which had been the Saturday of the Whitsun weekend. The crowds that poured into London for a preview of the decorations caught the police and the authorities unprepared. By late afternoon it was estimated that there were a million people on the procession route. The stands were thrown open to relieve the pressure and to give people the chance to sit down and rest.

From then on the coronation souvenir sellers began doing a roaring trade. A coronation souvenirs committee had been set up, purely as an advisory body, but to try to ensure that there were no errors and to persuade a high standard of souvenirs. The committee was responsible for the thousands of coronation presentation medals struck for local authorities to distribute to schoolchildren. It was hoped that with the committee's guidance the kind of wholesale error that had happened at the previous coronation would be

The Queen's bodyguard of the honourable corps of gentlemen at arms arrive for one of the numerous coronation rehearsals.

This London street was a front page picture on the eve of the coronation. On average, the residents of the cul-de-sac had contributed over a third of their weekly income for coronation decorations. But the house in the bottom left hand corner of this picture contributed nothing. It was occupied by the police. This was Rillington Place, notorious because of its connection with the Christie murders case.

avoided. Mugs made with the head of Edward VIII, in anticipation of his coronation, had flooded the market in an embarrassing way, either to be sold off cheaply or to be passed off to unsuspecting purchasers as George VI mugs.

Even so, in 1953 there was one error in many mugs and picture souvenirs that nobody seemed to notice at the time. In many of these Prince Philip was shown as a Commander, although he had been promoted to the rank of Admiral of the Fleet too late for the trade to depict him in the correct uniform.

On Wednesday 27 May, with the coronation then only a week away, traffic throughout the West End finally came to a standstill. That afternoon at Scotland Yard a high-level conference decided that after the weekend only priority and public service traffic could be allowed within a two-mile radius of Westminster, if a complete traffic breakdown was to be averted.

There was a row blowing up that day about the arrangements that had been made for schoolchildren to see the procession. Space – at 2.6 square feet per child – had been allocated for 33,000 secondary-school children along the Embankment. The London County Council, and the Middlesex, Essex, Hertfordshire and Croydon Councils were bearing the cost of £12,000 for the 28,000 children from their areas. But Kent was asking parents to pay six shillings for a child, West Ham seven shillings, East Ham seven shillings and sixpence and Surrey ten shillings.

On that day, too, Prince Philip was to inspect colonial troops who would be marching in the coronation procession. The inspection was to take place at the Royal Artillery barracks at Woolwich. But it was a day tight with engagements, notably the luncheon with the Queen at Westminster Hall given by the Commonwealth Parliamentary Association. Moreover the traffic situation was becoming critical. So a helicopter came down on to the lawn of Buckingham Palace to make the journey no more than a ten-minute hop. It was the Prince's second such helicopter flight and, in 1953, it was one of those incidental events that caught the attention of the public.

The next day details were released about the floodlighting that the Queen would switch on as dusk fell on coronation night. At St Ives they were hastily rearranging *their* coronation night firework display from the lakeside of the park where it was to have been, to a car park – the reason, nine cygnets had been hatched out at the lake.

There was a garden party at Buckingham Palace for Commonwealth guests. The new Broadway musical, *Guys and Dolls*, had its glittering first

Cheap, shoddy souvenirs, tasteless in their design and not commemorative of a great occasion created a problem which gave rise to the formation of a coronation souvenirs committee to 'advise and persuade'. The committee had three private categories – good, bad and horrible. These are three of the approved souvenirs.

For months before the occasion coronation hair styles were a gimmick in Britain. But it was one aspect of exploitation that spread throughout the whole world of women's fashion. This Austrian coronation hair style was being publicized by a Viennese coiffeur, in the spring of 1953.

The Coronation Souvenirs
Committee of the Council of
Industrial Design selected some
souvenirs for special merit
awards because they were
particularly well designed.
This low wattage night light
with a filament forming a
crown and the cypher 'E.R.'
was one of these.

Thousands of coronation
presentation medals were
struck for local authorities to
distribute to school children. It
was one of these medals that
the Queen pinned on Prince
Charles when she returned
from the Abbey – his first
decoration.

night at the Coliseum, and Josephine Baker was the night-life star of coronation week at the new Don Juan club.

On Friday 29 May, as coronation weekend began, London was beginning to burst at the seams. Every bed in every hotel was booked as liners, aircraft and trains brought the flood of visitors in from all over the world.

But it was not only the public who were creating an overcrowding problem. Quarters and catering had to be arranged for the officers and men taking part in the procession or lining the route – 16,100 from the army, 7,000 from the RAF, 3,600 from the navy, 2,000 from the Commonwealth countries and 500 from the colonies. Additionally there were 6,700 reserve and administrative troops, 1,000 military police and 7,000 police, seventy-five from provincial police forces brought in to help the London police. Altogether this was an army of 43,900 men. A tent city of 3,500 tents sprang up in Kensington Gardens for the troops from Pakistan and Malaya, for the Gurkhas and the regional police. The wartime military camps around London were reopened, as was the deep air-raid shelter at Clapham Common. The two big exhibition halls of Earl's Court and Olympia became mass dormitories. And on 29 May the British army hurled back a 6,000-strong enemy attack in Korea after a savage, six-hour, hand-to-hand battle for Hook Ridge, the key point of the Commonwealth front.

On that day, too, the first Comet airliner to fly the Atlantic landed at Uplands airport near Ottawa – after a 3,600-mile flight taking ten and a half hours, including brief refuelling stops at Keflavik in Iceland and Goose Bay, Labrador. The Comet was one of the three aircraft that gave Britain a coronation-year air supremacy. Neville Duke broke the world air speed record in a Hunter with a speed of 727.6 mph. Later Lieutenant-Commander Lithgow, in a Vickers Supermarine Swift, set up a new record of 737.7 mph.

The Queen's Beasts were set up outside the Abbey on 29 May. At the rehearsal that day, a crowd of 5,000 outside the Abbey and 2,000 in the Abbey saw the first of Norman Hartnell's 'secret' coronation dresses – worn by the maids of honour, Lady Jane Vane-Tempest-Stewart, Lady Moyra Hamilton and Lady Anne Coke, who were seen in their full coronation finery as they left the Abbey. There was one casualty. The Lyon King of Arms, one of the heralds, Sir Thomas Innes, collapsed and had to be taken back to his hotel by ambulance.

That night there were more tour coaches, in from the Home Counties to see the lights and decorations, than there were London buses on the streets. And that night the Queen attended a brilliant, all-night pre-coronation ball

A Souvenir
of the Coronation of

HER MAJESTY QUEEN ELIZABETH II
1953

Throughout the year of 1953 everything possible was linked with the coronation. A special presentation holder was issued for a coronation year National Savings gift token.

at Hampton Court, given by her Household Brigade. There were 2,000 guests at Hampton Court Palace, but along the road from Kingston and outside the Palace more than 40,000 people waited for over two hours. And when the Queen, with Princess Margaret and the Duke of Edinburgh beside her, saw all those people, she ordered the car's interior lights to be switched on, and its speed to be reduced. That night the first of the flowers for coronation day arrived at Heathrow – forty huge boxes of them from Australia, to decorate Parliament Square.

On 30 May the Duke of Edinburgh, in the new uniform of Admiral of the Fleet, had his first appointment of a crowded day, in pouring rain at Westminster Pier – with a salute, a handshake and two kisses. The salute and the handshake were for Prince Olav of Norway, and the kisses in the rain were for Crown Princess Martha and her daughter, Princess Astrid. The Norwegian royal family had stayed the night on board their royal yacht *Norge*, moored in the Pool of London.

By the end of that day the Duke had shaken hands with or kissed over 200 foreign royalty and distinguished guests. Foreign princes, rajahs, sheikhs, ministers of foreign governments and other national representatives, had rendezvoused in Paris to come to Britain as a party, crossing the Channel in a specially chartered ferry, the *Maid of Orleans*, and then travelling to Victoria Station on the Coronation Special. The last handshake of the day was with Jack Durrant, the driver of the train, a Dover man. Driver Durrant, who had not expected to be in the royal line-up, looked for a rag to clean his oily hands. 'Never mind about that,' said the Duke. Among the royalty arriving that day were Prince Axel of Denmark, Crown Prince Akihito of Japan, Prince Bertil of Sweden, Prince George of Greece, Prince Chula of Thailand, the Crown Prince of Ethiopia, and Prince Bernhard of the Netherlands who flew his own aircraft into Heathrow to be met by the Duke of Gloucester and the Duke of Kent.

The Coronation Stone had now been taken from the vaults and was in place under the Coronation Chair, and Special Branch men were mounting a day-and-night guard on it. And on 30 May Scotland Yard chiefs gave a final briefing to the 3,000 detectives whose job it was to guard London against the coronation criminals. These detectives had the trickiest of jobs and one gang of raiders caused a lot of red faces at Scotland Yard. Some of the Duke of Sutherland's house guests had to wear paste jewellery at the coronation because, on the night of 1 June, raiders made a swoop on the Duke's home in Wilton Crescent, Knightsbridge. They got away with gems belonging to the Duchess and guests worth between £40,000 and £50,000.

The full state harness. Herbert Croft, who had worked in the Royal Mews for nearly forty years, holds a horse's bridle bearing the Star of India.

This young couple, along with over half a million other people, settled down for a cold, wet night on the pavements of London on the eve of coronation day.

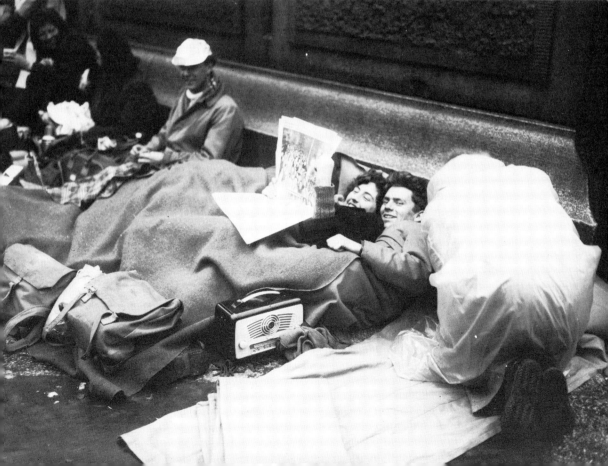

The theft was not discovered until the party was preparing to leave for the Abbey.

One other visitor's arrival at Heathrow was reported on 30 May. She was Maggie Port. She was seventy-seven, an English-born Toronto char-woman, and her employers were meeting the £170 cost of her trip back home for the coronation.

In many ways, Saturday 30 May was coronation eve. For the whole of that day the West End was one huge mass of people – a pageant of costume and uniform from every corner of the Commonwealth. It was a pheno-menon belonging to its own moment of time, unique and unrepeatable.

On Sunday 31 May at 3 pm, eighteen-year-old Anne Frances Passey from Surrey sat down at the kerbside in the Mall. But she had been beaten into first place as the first person to take up position to watch the coronation by seventy-three-year-old Mrs Zoe Neame, who had started her vigil at 8 am on that cold Sunday morning in Trafalgar Square. Mrs Neame had come down from her home in Buckinghamshire two weeks earlier to decide where to take up her position. She was no stranger to this odd business, having watched every royal ceremonial parade since 1921. She had been training for six months, toughening up for her wait whenever it rained she had been going out into her garden, just to get used to being soaked. And the Air Ministry weather office forecast for the next two days in-dicated that Mrs Neame had done exactly the right kind of training.

On that Sunday William Hepburn, aged sixty-four, of New Lodge, Hyde Park, collapsed and died – a few hours before his name was to appear in the coronation honours list in which he was made a member of the Royal Victorian Order for personal services to the Queen. He was the superin-tendent of the Royal Parks, and in the flower beds and glasshouses he con-trolled had been grown 77,000 red, white and blue plants to deck London on the coronation day he did not live to see.

Several hundred sightseers outside Marlborough House, including East Enders and overseas visitors were hardly able to believe their ears when the Queen's priest-in-waiting came out and said: 'Do come in to morning ser-vice in our chapel – the Queen will be delighted to have you.' They crowded in, not quite believing that this was a pre-coronation royal occasion, but no sooner had they filled the pews than they were joined by the Queen, the Queen Mother and the Duke for a simple Sunday service.

By midnight on Sunday people had driven their cars off many of the West End streets and with every hour more and more people with rugs, raincoats and provisions for the forty-hour wait were taking up positions along the

Modern communications techniques eliminated the possibilities of the confusions that had marred coronations in the past. This signal control point at the Queen Victoria Memorial opposite Buckingham Palace was one of fifteen that monitored the world's greatest pageant and controlled its progress.

procession route. There were medical students who had hitch-hiked from Edinburgh, there were young schoolgirls, there was a man from Sittingbourne with a supply of rum, eggs and milk, sufficient for the thirty rum flips he anticipated would see him through the wait, and in the Mall there was sixty-year-old Nellie Henderson from Belgrave Road, sw, whose third coronation this would be.

On Monday 1 June the coronation honours list was made exciting and dramatic by the knighthood of Gordon Richards. The little jockey from Shropshire had ridden 4,662 winners and he had become the first jockey ever to be knighted in what was Derby week as well as coronation week. A royal Derby victory would be a triumphant end to coronation week and the Queen's horse, Aureole, was joint favourite. But the joint favourite with the Queen's colt was Pinza. And Pinza was being ridden by Gordon Richards, who had never won a Derby and who was probably having his last chance before his already rumoured retirement. In the event the Derby winner of 1953 was ridden by Sir Gordon Richards.

The cricketer Jack Hobbs was knighted in the same honours list, as were John Gielgud the actor, and T. O. M. Sopwith, who was building the air speed record-breaking RAF Hawker Hunter jet fighters. And no knighthood announced on the eve of the coronation was more appropriate than that given to David Eccles who had had the courage to employ the then controversial modern architect, Sir Hugh Casson, to design the decorations that had transformed blitz-scarred London into a city of unforgettable momentary beauty.

On that Monday, in the hours before dawn, Special Branch detectives moved into the final, tense phase of their behind-the-scenes activities. Already, by now, the eight miles of pavements with temporary protective barriers were filling up. Because they had to seem no different from everybody else, now Scotland Yard women detectives took up their places too – with their raincoats, baskets of food, vacuum flasks and knitting. Now, too, some of the programme sellers were plain clothes men.

At 7.30 am a canvas-hooded lorry travelled down Regent Street, round Trafalgar Square and down Whitehall. Both the car just ahead of it and the one behind it contained some of the twenty picked Special Branch men who were smuggling 20 million pounds' worth of Crown Jewels from the Goldsmiths and Silversmiths Co., where they had been cleaned, to the Abbey. The drab-looking van swung into the Dean's Yard entrance to the Abbey, and the jewellery was then taken to the Jerusalem Chamber to be guarded by Yeoman Warders from the Tower of London until the Tuesday

When Henry III had rebuilt 'St Edward's Church' and created the Westminster Abbey that has survived the past seven centuries, it was built around a 'theatre' for the crowning of English Monarchs. On the night of 1 June 1953, on the eve of the coronation of Elizabeth II, this photograph of a 'stage' set for the solemn ceremony of a crowning on the next day, taken from a TV camera position, showed the scene as no human eye had ever seen it before. Central, on the raised dais, is the throne. To the left of this are the chairs for the three Royal Dukes. In front of it is King Edward's Chair, beneath which is the Stone of Destiny. To the left, and in front ot this is the Chair of Estate, behind which is the Royal Gallery.

morning. Then, as one of the first of the coronation rituals in the Abbey, the jewels would be carried in procession first to the high altar and then to the regalia table in the Annexe.

Late that night the Special Branch began the most secret of all their jobs. Guided by workmen, they began a thorough search of the hidden under-world of giant sewers and cable tunnels which formed a network under the procession route. Every entrance to this underworld was to be under unceasing watch.

On this day an airline route record was set up by a BEA Viscount, averaging 305 mph on the first flight of a new daily service to Geneva. In Glasgow some publicans began celebrating the coronation by selling whisky at a shilling (5p) a nip and beer at sixpence (2½p) a pint – pre-war prices. The Transport and General Workers Union lifted their ban on London milkmen delivering milk before 7.30 am, and Londoners began getting their milk at 4 am. The bakers ran out of bread, and the shops ran out of cream crackers.

The meat ration was still, then, only two shillings' worth a week, but the Ministry of Food had granted eighty-two licences to roast oxen, the applicants having established that an ox had been roasted on previous coronations.

The 81,000-ton *Queen Mary*, making her fastest journey across the Atlantic since the war, in four days, fourteen hours, six minutes, brought 1,500 last-minute arrivals. The 40,000-ton *Ile de France* was making a fast dash into Plymouth. Four hundred of the world's wealthiest tourists arrived aboard the 34,000-ton *Caronia* at Southampton, on a £1,000-a-head 'coronation cruise'. Into Southampton, too, but on a flying boat, came twenty-four South African farmers who had transferred from the liner *Pretoria Castle* at Madeira to make sure of getting to London in time for the coronation procession.

Into the Thames that day steamed seven ships which would remain there as floating hotels for the duration of the festivities for their passengers. The two largest, the Dutch liners *Ryndam* and *Beendam* anchored down river near Gravesend. The others were anchored at Greenwich and London Docks.

At London Airport the traffic was, for those days, breathtaking. All air traffic records were broken, in a week during which 700 planes brought in 16,394 passengers, most of them from the USA.

British Railways were running 6,500 special trains into London from the provinces during the final twenty-four-hour build-up to the coronation. Six thousand coaches were converging on central London from all over the country. The seventy heavy, nine-foot barrier gates that were to shut off

For 30,000 soldiers the coronation procession rations were cheese and meat rolls, fruit cake, an apple, chocolate and barley sugar. Those lining the route were given their issue while on duty. This was the scene in Piccadilly.

A brief vision of black arrows hurtling across the cloud, in wings of twenty-four aircraft, the RAF Meteors screamed over the crowded Mall for the flypast timed for the Queen's first appearance on the balcony of Buckingham Palace.

the coronation route not just from traffic but from any surge of spectators, swung into position. Outside this area London Transport buses now terminated at sixteen special perimeter points – in the final hours on Tuesday morning, from 4.30 am up to 8.30 am, when if you had not got there it would be too late – they were scheduled to run 44,000 journeys on sixty-five routes.

By midnight 1,000 firemen and their fire engines were manning their stations on the other side of those road barriers, inside the shut-off processional area. At midnight an army of gas, electricity and telephone trouble-shooting engineer teams were on station. So were 8,500 Red Cross and St John's ambulance men. So were the nurses and doctors manning 150 casualty stations, each sited on an emergency perimeter route linking them to Westminster Hospital.

The refreshment tents set up in the Royal Parks and behind the stands were manned by the 30,000 catering staff. To supplement still rationed foods and to encourage spectators to bring their own sandwiches and flasks, everybody had been allocated an extra pound of sugar and an extra four ounces of margarine that week. One London baker made 3,500 extra loaves that morning. Four thousand breakfasts were to be prepared at the House of Commons. Thirty thousand soldiers were being issued with haversack rations of one cheese roll, one meat roll, one bar of chocolate, one slice of fruit cake, one apple and two ounces of barley sugar.

Early on that Monday morning it had still been possible to buy a thirty-five-guinea stand seat for seventy-five guineas. By that evening, even the spivs had nothing left to sell. A block booking of eighty-nine seats was made from Buckingham Palace for Her Majesty's Theatre, where the show was *Paint Your Wagon*. Every London theatre was booked solid that night, although there was no special rush for seats at the St Martin's, where a new Agatha Christie play seemed as if it might have quite a good run ahead of it. Nobody then knew that *The Mousetrap* would celebrate a jubilee of its own in another quarter of a century. At the still new Festival Hall, the seventy members of the Cambridge University Madrigal Society were giving a first performance of *A Garland for the Queen*, 'a bright festoon of ten choral songs' commissioned by the Arts Council ... preceded by five of the twenty-four madrigals in the famous set *The Triumphs of Oriana*, dedicated to Elizabeth I in 1598. At the big hotels, this was the night of the coronation dances. Prices ranged from twelve guineas a head at the Savoy, where Nöel Coward appeared, to five guineas at the Mayfair.

Among those privileged to go into the Abbey that day was a small group

He climbed the plinth of one of the Nelson's Column Lions, to settle down for the night in the drenching rain. Amid great good humour, a policeman eventually brought him 'down to earth'.

of seamstresses from West End dressmakers, taking their sewing machines into the Annexe where, on duty the next day, they would be in the wings of the greatest spectacle of the century. Their job would be emergency and last-minute alterations and repairs.

But Monday 1 June 1953, coronation eve, was the night when London belonged to the people. Defying the rain, even singing in the rain, they poured into London all day long to form a dense, slow-moving stream of humanity flowing along the procession route. They brought blankets and radios with them, they brought food and wine, sleeping bags and tents. They sat down, they lay down, and by 5 pm every inch of sitting or lying space in the Mall was occupied – in places they were already ten deep. By 7 pm there were 10,000 living on the pavement from Marble Arch to Hyde Park Corner. They were twenty deep in Trafalgar Square where one young man climbed the plinth of one of the lions next to Nelson's Column with a lightweight scaling ladder, and settled down for the night on one of its paws in the rain that was lashing down. By dusk half a million people were lining the route – 100,000 in the Mall and 50,000 in Trafalgar Square. At 2.30 am they made a city of umbrellas. There was a strong wind. The temperature was down to forty-five degrees. A bonfire had been lit in Green Park, and crowds were swarming round it for warmth. Girls at a YWCA marquee were serving tea. Some of the squatters had chicken and champagne. Between the showers they sang or slept. And some were wakened out of their sleep to be told the coronation-day news – Everest had been conquered by a thirty-four-year-old New Zealander, Edmund Hillary.

6

The Curtain Rises

CORONATION DAY BEGAN AT 3.55 am for Major George Hopkins, superintendent of the Royal Mews. The eight Greys, mostly twelve-year-olds, that were to draw the Queen's golden coach had had their manes plaited the previous evening. But the major and his staff had a long job still ahead of them, and the harnessing that was scheduled to begin at 4.15 am was at the top of the entire coronation-day timetable. It would take nearly six hours to harness and prepare the Greys for their 10 am departure from the mews.

At 5 am, Tedder and McCreery (the leaders), Noah and Tipperary (second pair), Tovey and Show White (third pair), and Cunningham and Eisenhower, the last pair, had their breakfast of grain, hay and water. It would be their last meal for at least ten hours, a long time for horses to go without food.

At 5 am the Earl Marshal arrived at the Abbey. At 5.30 am the reporters and cameramen began to take up their places in the Abbey – hidden places, and with cameras concealed everywhere. Many of the reporters in an area high above Poets' Corner were to say afterwards that they could have done a much better job if they could only have watched the ceremony on TV. The key position, however was at the east end of the upper gallery, where had been built in all the equipment for the two most important TV cameras, and a commentary position for Richard Dimbleby, the French and Canadian radio commentators, and BBC sound commentators John Snagge and Howard Marshall. One group of cameras was concealed in the fourteenth-century tombs of Aylmer de Valence and Edmund Crouchback, only a few yards from where the Queen would be crowned. The 'hide' had been sound-proofed but the cameramen had to stand on the effigies. There were camera peepholes in the south transept and there had been a rehearsal for the cameramen on the Friday. That had taken only an hour and a half, and Bill Jordan of Pathé, who was just back from Korea, said it had been a much

A contrast in uniform and occasion – the policewoman was on duty, the nurse, waiting with her camera for the procession to pass by, was not.

The typical front page that told it all – the crowds waiting overnight in the rain, the conquest of Everest, the Derby favourite odds – and the dress that was every woman's talking point on that day of Tuesday 2 June 1953.

OVERLEAF The coronation procession viewed from Buckingham Palace. The State Coach is passing round the Victoria Memorial, where the crowds have a birds-eye view.

more comfortable job covering the war. His particular camera hide had to be reached by steps at the back of the altar. Once he was in position just after 6 am he had to stay there, sitting and crouching, with only three feet of head room, for eight hours. Jordan told the *Daily Express*'s Bernard Wickstead, who had been at Nyeri when the news of George VI's death had broken and who was now to climb up to the ceiling of the Abbey to see the crowning, 'After eight hours of it I doubt if I will ever stand straight again.'

At 6 am food from Buckingham Palace arrived. The two footmen carrying it were not allowed to take it into the Abbey. Nobody had provided them with the necessary passes. At 6.05 the Earl Marshal, an overcoat over his white breeches and wearing brown carpet slippers, made an appearance. A Gold Stick usher, in velvet, was summoned. The iron barrier across the peers' entrance was removed and the usher helped a Palace butler, who had now arrived, to carry the hamper of food from the Palace into the Annexe.

By seven o'clock the Abbey was beginning to fill up – the peers not taking part in the procession in the south transept, the peeresses in the north transept. All of them were seated in rows by order of precedence – the dukes behind the three chairs that would be occupied by the royal dukes, then the marquesses, then the earls and viscounts and finally the barons; and then, behind them, privileged to be present but to see little, the commoners. At about 7.30 am, in a room at the back of Buckingham Palace that overlooks the lawns and the flower beds and the lake, the Queen was brought her morning tea and orange juice. By eight o'clock the Annexe of the Abbey was filling up with dukes, earls, generals and field-marshals. At 8.57 the first members of the royal family arrived – Lord and Lady Harewood with Gerald Lascelles.

There were to be nine separate processions to the Abbey, and one big cavalcade from the Abbey after the ceremony. But at nine o'clock, when many people had already been in the Abbey for three hours, it was still an hour and a quarter before the Queen's procession would leave Buckingham Palace. The Queen and her husband had had a light breakfast together at 8.30, and now she was being dressed. At 9.30 a buffet was opened in the Annexe and a queue formed – possibly the most brilliantly robed queue, with more titles and famous names in it, than any other queue in the history of the country. Right at its head was the Bishop of London. And unobtrusively the cleaners were already quietly vacuuming the carpets.

At 10.15 the Queen, accompanied by the Duke of Edinburgh, walked down the red-carpeted steps from the grand entrance of the Palace to enter the State Coach. It was, for them, the climax to eighteen months of personal involvement in the planning that lay far behind the carpenters and the seam-

The Duchess of Kent on her way to the Abbey with her son, the Duke of Kent.

OVERLEAF A section of Her Majesty's procession, led by members of the Air Council, making its way through Admiralty Arch, and past Trafalgar Square en route for Westminster Abbey.

stresses, the technicians and the bishops, the Minister of Works, the court of claims and the Earl Marshal. There had been, for instance the question of the Duke's role in the processions. Should he travel to the Abbey in a separate coach? Or should he, indeed, ride on horseback? Or should they travel together in the State Coach? The only precedent of a Queen regnant with a prince consort had been that of Queen Anne and her husband Prince George of Denmark – but it provided no precedent for the coronation procession of 1953. Queen Anne had suffered so badly from gout that she had had to be carried to the Abbey in a low chair. It had been wisely decided that the precedent to be created was that Queen and prince consort should, as husband and wife, travel together.

When they left they were watched, from an upper room, by Prince Charles, Princess Anne and fifty other children invited by the Queen to see her leaving for the coronation. Prince Charles would later be driven in a car by a back route to the Abbey, and taken through back corridors to join his grandmother in the royal gallery in time to witness the actual crowning ceremony.

At 10.16, a minute after the Queen was beginning to leave the Palace, a royal family procession arrived at the Abbey. It included the Duchess of Kent, the Duchess of Gloucester and the Princess Royal. It was five minutes late, in a timetable which could not afford any disorganization of schedules, and they rushed into the Abbey. Of course, there were moments when disaster seemed to threaten. The Duke of Beaufort's coronet was lost – a few minutes before he was due to enter the Abbey from the Annexe in the Queen's procession. And the biggest near-disaster of the day was when, just before the State Coach was due to come into view for a television audience of 27 million people, the BBC control room experienced a complete failure on sound due to a power link breakdown. It turned out to be a faulty lead and was repaired only a minute or two before Sylvia Peters introduced the programme at 10.15 from 'outside Buckingham Palace'. The State Coach left the Palace at 10.26.

At 10.37 Princess Margaret and the Queen Mother entered the Annexe having arrived in a procession from Clarence House in the Irish State Coach. And now with still nearly an hour before the Queen would enter from the Annexe the processions from the Annexe into the Abbey were taking place. The procession of royal and other representatives of foreign states was led by Bluemantle and Rouge Croix Pursuivants to the choir area below the enthronement theatre. And among the foreign princes were the American George Marshall, the Frenchman Bidault and the Russian Yakob Alexandrovitch Malik. This long procession, the end of which was still forming up

The Duchess of
Gloucester,
accompanied by her
sons, Prince William
and Prince Richard,
leaving her carriage to
enter the Abbey.

in the Annexe while its vanguard were taking their seats on either side of the processional aisle, involved the representatives of over seventy states wearing every imaginable kind of uniform and ceremonial dress.

The next procession was that of the rulers of states under the Queen's protection, led by Rouge Dragon and Portcullis Pursuivants – a small procession of half a dozen sultans, their costumes glittering with jewels, which included the fabulous figure of the tallest queen in the world – 6ft-3in. Queen Salote of Tonga wearing her incredibly dramatic headdress of twin egret feathers, which a reporter described as 'two thin sticks with a dried flower decoration'.

Next the Dean and Prebendaries came in their procession from the Jerusalem Chamber where they had assembled. As they appeared the choir began the Tallis litany, and with the litany and its responses from the congregation already assembled, the coronation service had begun. As the clerics took their seats the real ceremonial began with the procession into the Abbey from the Annexe of the princes and princesses of the blood royal – the Princess Royal, the Duchesses of Gloucester and Kent with their sons, and Princess Alexandra. They had made up the lost five minutes' delay in reaching the Abbey on time and the Earl Marshal's timetable was running like clockwork.

Then came the first moment containing the drama of emotion – the procession of the Queen Mother who, sixteen years before, had been herself crowned Queen in this place and at such a ceremony. With her younger daughter, her procession from Clarence House had used the Irish State Coach. The Somerset and Windsor Heralds led this procession. Princess Margaret followed them. Then came the Heralds of Richmond, York, Chester and Lancaster, and finally the Queen Mother in a gown of white satin embroidered in gold and silver, over which she wore the Blue Riband of the Garter.

Now came a pause in the Abbey. In the Annexe the Queen's procession was already forming up behind the Abbey Beadle, who would lead it. Behind him the Abbey canons were formed up, behind them the Dean of Westminster wearing the velvet cope which was first worn at the coronation of Charles II. And they, and all behind them, were now waiting for the Queen, whose progress from Buckingham Palace was being reported to the Annexe from each checkpoint she passed. In the past there had been many blunders, some bordering upon the ridiculous, at coronations, and in 1761 the start of the Abbey service was delayed for a whole hour, and the subsequent banquet at Westminster Hall started in stumbling, blundering darkness as a consequence. Modern communications techniques give historians

Queen Salote of Tonga leaves Buckingham Palace. One of the most colourful figures in the procession, Queen Salote won great admiration from the crowds by refusing to have the roof of her carriage raised, and smiling gaily throughout, in spite of the torrential rain.

no occasion for impish reporting. The 1953 coronation was going like clockwork. Though it is true that at 11.05 am the Earl Marshal sent a message
to the Duke of Gloucester urging him to hurry up with his robing.

When the Queen left Buckingham Palace the first of her subjects to see
and greet her were the holders of the Victoria Cross and disabled ex-service-
men. They had started the cheering that became a flowing tide of sound
down the Mall, through Admiralty Arch, down Northumberland Avenue,
along the Victoria Embankment where the schoolchildren were – an addition to the route made at the Queen's request so that they might have their
own place – up Bridge Street and round Parliament Square.

Altogether twenty bands were along the full procession route that day
and another twenty-nine bands were in the full procession. Now, together
with the tide of the cheering, the bands in the Queen's procession and those
along the route, told those waiting inside the Abbey of the progress of her
approach. The tumult could be heard above the organ music. At 11.10 the
tumult died. The long, slow-moving Queen's procession now began to flow
into the Abbey from the Annexe, led by the Abbey's own dignitaries –
the Beadle, the canons in their scarlet, and the Dean with the Cross of Westminster carried high. Then, as the trumpets sounded, came the colourful
procession dictated in its form and order by traditions and customs some
of which dated back more than eight centuries. Six Pursuivants, three
abreast, carrying the batons of their office, led the orders of knighthood with
their brilliant mantles of pink, grey, blue, red and crimson. Next the high
commissioners of the Commonwealth carrying their standards to give them
to the scarlet-cloaked barons of the Cinque Ports in a part of the ceremony
that was new on this occasion.

Then came the other standards. The Union Standard carried by Captain
J. L. M. Dymoke whose ancestors had been the sovereign's Champion at
earlier coronations. The Standard of the Principality of Wales carried by
Lord Harlech. The Standards of the Quarterings of the Royal Arms; the
harp of Ireland carried by Lord de L'Isle and Dudley, the lion of Scotland
carried by Viscount Dudhope, the leopards of England carried by the Earl
of Derby. And finally the Royal Standard carried by Viscount Montgomery
wearing the Garter mantle over his field-marshal's uniform.

The standard-bearers were followed by the bearer of the first pieces of
the regalia to be carried in the procession – the Ring, the Armillae and the
Sword for the Offering carried by Lord Hardinge. Now came two more
Pursuivants leading the four Knights of the Garter – Viscount Allendale,
the Duke of Wellington, Earl Fortescue and the Duke of Portland – who

The band of the Grenadier Guards leaving Buckingham Palace.

would hold the canopy for the anointing. After them were the seven Commonwealth prime ministers, followed by Sir Winston Churchill in the uniform of Lord Warden of the Cinque Ports, over which he had the mantle of the Garter. Next appeared the Cross of York, followed by the Archbishop of York; the Lord High Chancellor in wig and damask and gold robe; and his Purse Bearer carrying the tasseled purse which, in the days when the ritual had been introduced, had contained the Great Seal of England. Finally, in this section of the procession, came the High Cross of Canterbury, followed by the Archbishop of Canterbury and his retinue of chaplains.

Like a punctuation mark, there was a slight gap in the procession, followed by the Heralds and the Lyon King of Arms, leading the Duke of Edinburgh, wearing a robe of scarlet velvet over his uniform as Admiral of the Fleet. On each side of him walked four Gentlemen at Arms wearing high plumes and carrying axes. He was to take his place in front of the first row of peers at the head of the south transept, with the Dukes of Gloucester and Kent on his left. This was to be his place until he would be the first after the Archbishop of Canterbury to pay homage to the newly-crowned Queen, and to become only the second royal husband in all of English history to have paid such homage to his wife. By the precedent also set at the coronation of Queen Anne, as Queen regnant's husband, the Duke preceded the main procession of the regalia – St Edward's Staff carried by the Earl of Ancaster: the Sceptre with the Cross carried by Viscount Portal: the Spurs, carried by Lord Hastings and Lord Churston, each bearing a scarlet cushion; the Swords of Temporal Justice, of Spiritual Justice, and of Mercy, carried by the Duke of Buccleuch and Queensberry, the Earl of Home and the Duke of Northumberland.

Then came the Kings of Arms carrying their crowns, and the Lord Mayor of London, carrying the Crystal Sceptre of the City. Next followed the Earl Marshal with the Marquess of Salisbury, carrying in front of him the great Sword of State. After them was the Lord High Steward, Viscount Cunningham, carrying St Edward's Crown with which the Queen would be crowned. On either side of him were the Duke of Richmond and Gordon carrying the Rod with the Dove, and Earl Alexander of Tunis carrying the Orb. Immediately behind them followed three bishops carrying the paten (the shallow dish used for bread at eucharist), the Bible and the chalice.

And then the 'punctuation' in the procession was not just a brief interval in spacing, but a momentary silence between the ending of the singing of the choir and the sudden great ringing cry of the Westminster schoolboys: '*Vivat Regina! Vivat Regina Elizabetha. Vivat! Vivat! Vivat!*' In the roots of

Second in splendour only to the State Coach, the Golden Coach of the Lord Mayor of London, bearing the coronation year Lord Mayor, Sir Rupert de la Bere, passing along the Embankment on the way to the Abbey.

Drawn by brewery horses, and the heaviest of all the coaches in the procession, this was the Speaker's Coach leaving the House of Commons for the shortest of all the journeys to the Abbey.

Colonial troops march past the statue of Eros, encased in an ornate
golden cage for the celebrations.

language Latin, the language first of the Latini and then of the Romans, belongs as much to the French, the Spanish and the English as it does to the Italians. It is the language of the church, of medicine, of botany, of the sciences, of the arts, of traditions that go back everywhere in the Old World to the beginnings of culture. And the cry: *'Vivat! Vivat! Vivat!'*, echoing through Westminster Abbey as it had done in recognition of thirty-seven sovereigns before her at their coronations, was one of the most emotionally stirring moments of the coronation of Elizabeth II as it orchestrated the entrance from the Annexe of a young queen coming to her crowning.

At no other time in the history of the world, because of the unique combination of circumstance and technology, had any other human being been so completely exposed to the thoughts, the understanding, the responses and reactions of so many other people. For two and a half hours the whole world looked at Elizabeth II and she was alone with that knowledge. All the emperors and empresses, kings and queens, conquerors, rulers, dictators of the past had had their moments of greatness on little stages. Suddenly, for that young woman of twenty-six, that stage had become incredibly vast. She was not upon this lonely stage, before the biggest audience ever known, because of personal choice, or ambition, or a chosen profession, but because of the inescapable destiny of her birth. And it is a matter far above politics, or tradition, or rituals – that Elizabeth, the daughter of George VI and the wife of Philip, commanded not just the homage of her liegemen, but the respect and admiration of men such as Yakob Alexandrovitch Malik, who was there to witness what his country had perhaps sacrificed when they rejected the evolutionary development of a monarchical society.

The Queen was, from the moment of her entry into the Abbey with six silver-gowned maids of honour supporting her twenty-foot train, superb – and there were over 27 million witnesses to the fact! Neither history in the reality, nor the histrionics of stage or screen in the simulation of reality, had ever given, not just the British Commonwealth but the whole world, a woman quite like this.

The procession, watched by the entire country, came up to the theatre of enthronement. The Queen approached and faced the altar beyond the throne. The Archbishop of Canterbury bowed to her. She moved to the Chair of Estate in front of the royal gallery and knelt for a brief period of private prayer. And some of the congregation in the Abbey and all of the television audience watched the young Queen at her prayers. The few who perhaps used their imaginations about the nature of her prayers made the intrusiveness of the cameras very well worthwhile.

The Queen and the Duke of Edinburgh enter the Abbey via the Annexe.

Now, piece by piece, the regalia passed from the Archbishop, to whom their bearers had presented them, to the Dean of Westminster who laid them on the altar, temporal power being symbolically submitted to spiritual power. Next, the Queen moved to King Edward's Chair, her maids of honour spreading her train out behind her, a great splash of crimson on gold. The mitred Archbishop of Canterbury, flanked by the four Great Officers of State, carrying his Cross, came from the altar to face first east from the theatre, then south, then west, then north. Each time he gave the ritualistic announcement calling for consent and recognition. It dated back to pagan days when the elected chieftain, shown by the shield-carrying ritual, had been presented to his tribe for consent of loyalty. At each presentation the Archbishop's voice demanded an answer. 'Sirs, I here present unto you Queen Elizabeth, your undoubted Queen, wherefore, all you who are come this day to do your homage and service, are you willing to do the same?' From east, south, west and north, in turn, came the acclamation: 'God Save Queen Elizabeth.'

Now, with the Bishops of Durham and of Bath and Wells, 'supporting' her on either side, the Queen, attended by her maids of honour and by the Officers of State with Swords, returned to the Chair of Estate. The Archbishop of Canterbury now administered the oath. 'Madam! Is Your Majesty willing to take the Oath?' For the first time the Queen spoke, and for the first time a sovereign spoke to the entire nation. 'I am willing.' The oath commits the sovereign to the observance of rights established by centuries of conflict between church and monarchy. This conflict was once very serious, but in the mid-twentieth century the importance of the oath has become that of a factor of stability in society. The Queen, preceded by the Sword of State, now went to the altar and knelt there with her hand resting on the opened Bible and made her formal affirmation, kissing the Bible and signing an engrossed copy of the oath on vellum. She then returned to the Chair of Estate.

Now the Moderator of the General Assembly of the Church of Scotland played his part in the ceremonials. Sombrely gowned among so much splendour, he took the Bible from the Dean and, as the Archbishop invited her to accept it, proclaimed it to her as a source of wisdom. The service now developed through minor rituals towards the great sacramental phase of the ceremony – the anointing. The Archbishop went to the altar to lay his hands on the Ampulla which held the oil for the anointing. The voices of the choir rang out the words of Handel's *Zadok the Priest*, composed for the coronation of George II. But although the music was Handel's, the words

The procession of the regalia through the cloisters of Westminster Abbey. First comes the paten and chalice, followed by the Holy Bible, and finally the Imperial State Crown.

The Queen looks serious as she prepares for the long and demanding coronation ceremony. Her maids of honour arrange the magnificent robe of purple velvet.

OVERLEAF Seated in the St Edward's Chair, and wearing the simple white garment over the glittering coronation dress, the Queen prepares for the solemn ceremony of anointing. The television and film cameras were turned away for this part of the ceremony.

go back in records 750 years before the anointing of King Edgar in 973, and unquestionably long before that: 'Zadok the priest and Nathan the prophet anointed Solomon King; and all the people rejoiced and said: God save the king, Long live the king, May the king live forever ...' Zadok was the son of Ahitub, of the House of Eleazar. He was a priest in the reign of David. Abiathar was the High Priest in the time of Solomon, but Solomon set him aside and made Zadok the High Priest. Solomon was anointed by Zadok in the year 1015 BC, a Jew who married the daughter of an Egyptian Pharaoh. Nearly 3000 years later the name of Zadok was being heard by television and radio audiences all over the world on the occasion of a coronation anointing not altogether dissimilar in ritual to his anointment of Solomon and completely identifiable in meaning.

Now, as the Archbishop invoked a blessing upon the Oil, the Queen raised her hands and lifted the diadem from her head and handed it to the Mistress of the Robes. The Lord Great Chamberlain moved forward to assist in divesting her of the Royal Robe. The maids of honour folded it and gave it into the arms of the Groom of the Robes. The Collar of the Garter was removed and a simple white garment was put on the Queen over the splendid coronation dress.

As the Queen moved to her place in King Edward's Chair, Prince Charles' nurse, Helen Lightbody, was bringing him into the royal gallery. The Officers of Arms now carried the richly embroidered canopy of cloth of gold supported on four silver staffs, and the four Knights of the Garter came forward to hold it over the chair and the Queen to screen the ceremony of the anointing from view. And at this point the TV and film cameras in the Abbey were turned away from the scene. The Dean of Westminster carried the eagle-shaped Ampulla from the altar. He poured a little oil from its beak into the anointing spoon. The Archbishop took the oil on his fingers and was heard to say: 'Be thy Hands anointed with holy Oil. Be thy Breast anointed with holy Oil. Be thy Head anointed with holy Oil; as kings, priests and prophets were anointed. And as Solomon was anointed king by Zadok the priest and Nathan the prophet, so be thou anointed, blessed and consecrated Queen over the Peoples, whom the Lord thy God hath given thee to rule and govern.' The Dean then returned the Ampulla and Spoon to the altar, the Queen knelt and the Archbishop said a blessing over her. The canopy was moved away and now began the impressive investiture with all the symbols of sovereignty.

First, assisted by the Mistress of the Robes, the Dean of Westminster gowned the Queen in the white linen Colobium Sidonis. Next she was robed

Prince Charles was brought to the Abbey by car by a back route and taken to the Royal Gallery to be a witness of the ceremony of his mother's crowning. This unique photograph shows a future king having his first lesson in Monarchy from his grandmother, the Queen Mother, while his aunt, Princess Margaret watches.

in the golden Supertunica, which was fastened at her waist by its girdle. Seated again in the Chair, the Golden Spurs were brought to her by the Lord Great Chamberlain, and she gave a token of acceptance by touching them before they were returned to the altar.

The Marquess of Salisbury gave the Great Sword of State to the Lord Chamberlain of the Household. In place of this he took the bejewelled Sword of the Offering. He carried this to the Archbishop, who took it to the altar to bless it. Then, with the Archbishop of York and the Bishops of London and Winchester, the Archbishop carried the sword and delivered it to the Queen with the enjoinment that with its power she should ensure justice. The Queen rose from her seat, robed as were the emperors of Byzantium but as yet wearing no crown and no headdress of any kind, and carried the jewelled Sword in the palms of her outstretched hands to the altar where it was laid.

When she returned to King Edward's Chair the Marquess of Salisbury took an embroidered bag containing one hundred newly minted shillings and gave this as a 'redemption' price for the sword. The Dean gave the Sword back to the Marquess. The Marquess drew the sword from its scabbard and moved back to stand on the Queen's right hand. By ritual he would now carry this sword naked throughout the rest of the ceremony.

Next the Armillae were brought from the Altar by the Dean and given to the Archbishop, who invested the Queen with them, putting them on to her wrists and reminding her of their symbolism as a bond uniting her to her peoples. The Groom of the Robes now came from the chapel behind the altar carrying the Royal Stole and giving this to the Dean. The Stole was placed around the Queen's neck and tied to her arms above the elbows. Then the Pallium, or Imperial Robe – a mantle of cloth of gold, heavily embroidered – was placed on her shoulders by the Dean, assisted by the Mistress of the Robes; the Lord Great Chamberlain fastened the clasps.

Seated again, the Queen now received, one by one, the jewelled pieces of the regalia as they were brought from the altar, the symbolism of each one being announced as it was delivered to her. First the Archbishop placed the Orb into her hand. Next he placed the Ring on the fourth finger of her right hand. Then Lord Woolton, as Chancellor of the Duchy of Lancaster, presented her with a richly embroidered white kid gauntlet glove – a symbolic reminder of the abolition of the Danegeld tax in 1163. Following this the two sceptres were brought from the altar. The Royal Sceptre, with its brilliant diamond, considered to be the most perfect stone in the world, was placed upright in her right hand and the Sceptre with the Dove

One of the most moving moments of the ceremony: Prince Philip pays homage to the newly-crowned Queen.

similarly placed in her left hand. All that remained now was the actual crowning.

Seated there, facing the altar, robed in gold, uncrowned and bareheaded, holding the ancient symbols of sovereignty, the Queen could only be seen by the bishops and archbishops on her left and from the royal gallery and the bearers of the regalia with positions just below the altar and in front of the royal gallery – and, of course, by some 27 million people watching television screens. Now the pages, in traditional costume, brought their coronets to the peers, and the peers and peeresses made themselves ready to put their coronets on. At the altar the archbishop lifted the St Edward's Crown for all the congregation to see as he invoked a blessing upon it.

The Archbishop, accompanied by the other bishops, then returned to the Queen. The Dean carefully placed the Crown on a scarlet cushion and carried it to the Archbishop. The Archbishop took it from the cushion, held it uplifted, then gently placed it on the Queen's head. 'At the sight thereof,' the form and order of the coronation laid down, 'the people with loud and repeated shouts shall cry: God save the Queen.' As the peers and peeresses put on their coronets, and the Kings of Arms put on their heraldic crowns, the acclamation rang out through the Abbey against a fanfare of trumpets. The bells began to ring. Distantly the guns being fired in salute at the Tower of London could be heard. Queen Elizabeth II had been crowned, seated on King Edward's Chair.

The bearers of the swords now formed a guard behind the throne for the enthronement ceremony. As the Lords formed up on the steps to the throne, the Queen faced the congregation and moved from King Edward's Chair to the throne. In the origins of the ceremony the newly crowned sovereign was enthroned by being physically lifted on to the throne by the bishops and peers. This is no longer done, but the bishops and peers turned their hands as the Queen mounted the five steps, symbolizing the 'lifting' as she seated herself. Now the scene was being set for the feudal ritual of the acts of homage.

A boy page, in the white-and-red livery of the Earl Marshal, approached the throne carrying a kneeling stool which he placed at the Queen's feet. Then he took up his position on the left of the steps to hold the scarlet cushion on which the peers would place their coronets when they approached to perform their acts of homage. The Queen passed the two sceptres to their bearers, and removed the Glove. First the Archbishop knelt on the stool before her, his hands between hers and swore his fidelity to her as sovereign, the

The Queen's procession leaves the Abbey. As she passed through the choir and nave, the great congregation sang the National Anthem.

assembled bishops repeating his words but substituting the names of their own diocese.

And then the Duke of Edinburgh led the procession of homage. Kneeling at her feet, he said: 'I, Philip, Duke of Edinburgh, do become your liege man of life and limb, and of earthly worship; and faith and truth I will bear unto you, to live and die, against all manner of folks. So help me, God.' As he rose, he touched the Crown and kissed the Queen's left cheek. He was followed by the other royal dukes, and then by the Duke of Norfolk. As the Earl Marshal recited the oath of homage, his words were repeated, after their own titles, by the dukes kneeling in the south transept. After the Duke of Norfolk, in turn, the senior in each next rank of the peerage – the Marquess of Huntley, the Earl of Shrewsbury, Viscount Arbuthnot and Baron Mowbray performed the act of homage, their oaths being repeated in each case by the peers of the same rank as themselves. The homage paid by Baron Mowbray ended the coronation, but the ritual of the ceremony was not yet over.

As the congregation joined in the singing of a hymn, the Queen left the throne, handed the sceptres to the Lord Great Chamberlain and took off her Crown. She then offered the bread and wine which were placed on the altar, and presented the gift of an altar cloth and a 'wedge of gold of a pound's weight'. The Duke of Edinburgh now joined her at the altar and, as they received communion, the cameras turned away for the second time during the service. After the communion she returned to the throne chair, again wearing the heavy St Edward's Crown and carrying the two sceptres. Here she remained for the conclusion of the religious service and the singing of the Te Deum. Then, preceded by the Archbishop and with the supporting bishops on each side of her, she moved in procession to St Edward's Chapel and passed from sight.

While she was in the Chapel the return procession was being marshalled by the pursuivants in the area of the theatre. The Queen herself was also preparing for this procession out of the Abbey and into the Annexe. The St Edward's Crown was replaced by the Imperial State Crown. The investment robes of Byzantium were replaced by the Robe of Purple Velvet which she could now wear as a crowned and consecrated monarch. As the first chords of the National Anthem were played, she reappeared from St Edward's Chapel, carrying the Sceptre with the Cross in her right hand and the Orb in her left, the long train of the Purple Velvet Robe being carried by her six maids of honour. The procession out of the Abbey began to move.

Carrying the Orb and Sceptre, and wearing the Imperial State Crown, the Queen
returns to the State Coach.

OVERLEAF One of the problems for peers was that of robes—owned, borrowed or
hired. The unanticipated problem was that of wearing such costume with dignity
in the inclement weather of 2 June 1953. Photography is not always kind to
historical tradition.

CORONATION

The Queen had entered the west door of the Abbey from the Annexe at 11.25. It was 1.50 pm when she returned to the Annexe, after a coronation ceremony which had lasted nearly two and a half hours. The Queen, the Duke and other members of the royal family were now able to retire to their annexe rooms for the luncheon that the Palace footmen had brought in a hamper at six o'clock that morning – smoked salmon, foie gras, sausage rolls and cheese and biscuits. To drink there was champagne and coffee. The family toasted the Queen in champagne. She drank only water. She stayed at the Abbey nearly a quarter of an hour longer than had been planned, and there was a rumour that Sir Winston Churchill persuaded her to delay the start of the great procession, saying: 'Wait a few minutes. I *know* that the sun is going to come out.'

Rain had fallen heavily and unceasingly for an hour and a half during the Abbey ceremony, and it was still pouring down when the great cavalcade of 13,000 troops, twenty-nine bands and twenty-seven carriages began the seven-mile route back to the Palace. The passengers travelling in the only four open carriages in the procession were, like the crowds, immediately drenched. At one point the crowds called to the sultans in their soaked robes: 'Put up your hoods.' And this was when the Queen of Tonga, in the last of the carriages with the Sultan of Kelantan, endeared herself in the memories of all who saw her that day by refusing to shelter. The head of the procession, led by Colonel B. J. O. Burrows of the War Office staff, followed immediately by four troopers of the Household Cavalry and then the first four bands, had already reached Stanhope Gate, Hyde Park, two miles away, when the Queen re-entered her coach and left the Abbey. And by then, the sun was shining for her departure.

The journey was timed to take an hour and forty minutes – and the whole procession took forty-five minutes to pass any given point along the route which toured the West End, taking in Piccadilly, the East Carriage Drive of Hyde Park parallel to Park Lane, Oxford Street to Oxford Circus, Regent's Street and Haymarket. It rained intermittently. The *blanco* on the sailors' caps and on the white helmets of some of the mounted troops, ran down the backs of their uniforms in tell-tale rivulets. Nobody seemed to mind. People in the shelter of the stands passed their umbrellas down to people on the pavement who were without protection. It was cold and wet, but it was never miserable. It was reported that in one area the people in the stands were giving three cheers for the people on the pavement, and the people on the pavement were giving three cheers for the people in the stands.

Princess Alice, Countess of Athlone, and the Duke of Beaufort leave the Abbey.
The Duke had experienced near disaster when his coronet was lost minutes before
he was due to enter the Abbey in the Queen's procession.

The fact was that it was a procession greater than any even London had ever seen before, and there were reasons to be found for cheering everybody in the procession, beginning with one of those very first bands, that of the 1st Battalion of the Gloucester Regiment because of the heroic stand the regiment had just made at Imjin in Korea. These bands were followed by the colonial contingents – the armed police forces of Cyprus, the Solomon Islands, Trinidad, the Bahamas, the Windward Islands, North Borneo, Sarawak and the Federation of Malaya. And close behind them colonial army, navy and air force detachments, contributing twenty-seven different uniforms – in all 490 men.

After them came the Commonwealth – seventy-five men from air, military and police forces in Rhodesia: seventy-five from naval, military and air forces in Ceylon; 182 men from Pakistan; 170 from South Africa; 175 from New Zealand; 270 from Australia; and 450 from Canada, including a loudly cheered detachment of the Mounties. Then four bands leading the RAF (1,922 men) and the Home Guard (100 men). Next came the army, with the pipe bands of the Scottish and Irish regiments and the pipers from Pakistan and Nepal. Seventy-five regiments of the British army were there, and the crowd gave a special roar of welcome for the eighty-four Gurkhas. The navy, headed by two bands of Royal Marines, followed the army. They were followed by the Foot Guards and after them came the King's Troop of the Royal Horse Artillery with their clattering gun carriages and chestnut horses.

The parade of the armed forces now gave way to the carriage processions, the first being that of the four open carriages of the colonial rulers, each with their own mounted escorts. Next came the closed Clarence coaches of the prime ministers, each with its own national escort, the last escort being the 4th Queen's Own Hussars for the carriage of Sir Winston and Lady Churchill.

But processions of such magnitude are inevitably vulnerable to casualties. In fact there were to be 6,873 casualties on the processional route, mostly of people fainting, although 313 were taken to hospital. Six soldiers were injured by fixed bayonets when their rear rank slipped. The Churchills were the only casualties in the procession itself, when their carriage was forced to a halt outside Canada House because of risk of collision with another carriage. Having lost his place in the procession, Churchill withdrew from it and drove straight to Downing Street.

The carriage procession of the princes and princesses of the blood royal followed – three carriages escorted by the Household Cavalry. Im-

Happy and not concealing her pride in her daughter's dignity throughout the long and tiring ceremony, Queen Elizabeth, the Queen Mother, leaving Westminster Abbey.

Leaving the Abbey after the ceremony, the Princess Royal (left), the Duke of Norfolk (centre) and Prince William of Gloucester (right).

Posterity need never question as exaggerated the report of heavy rainfall on coronation day. The patience and good-humour of the waiting crowd was tested to the full.

Among nearly seven thousand processional route incidents, the most notable was outside Canada House, when Sir Winston Churchill's coach became a casualty and retired from the procession. His coach and its escort is seen centre right, with the procession detouring round it.

mediately after them came the Queen Mother's procession, the House-hold Cavalry escort to the Irish State Coach carrying the Royal Standard.

RAF, army and navy chaplains and aides-de-camp formed the vanguard of the final phase of the procession which included Air Ministry, War Office and Admiralty staff; marshals of the RAF, field-marshals and admirals of the fleet; and then the colourful beginning of the climax to the procession – the Yeomen of the Guard, followed by a rare appearance of the Queen's Bargemaster and twelve Watermen and the first of four divisions of the Sovereign's Escort.

On some parts of the full procession route some people had been waiting for up to fifty-six hours on the pavement edge in wind and rain and cold that nobody had anticipated for a June day when the coronation date had been fixed. Over half a million people had been there overnight, for at least sixteen hours.

The great, deep thunder of the roar of acclamation which greeted the golden coach and its radiant passenger was a wave of sound that swept slowly through seven miles of London streets that day, and continued for nearly two hours. In all history, no multitude had ever made a greater sound than London made when the Queen's State Coach, drawn by the slow-moving clip-clopping eight Windsor Greys, went back to Buckingham Palace. This was what they had waited for – a million of them.

And as if she had an insight into what all the waiting had involved, and all that it meant, she made it worthwhile to every single one of them with her happy, smiling acknowledgment of their acclamation. The Queen's arrival back at Buckingham Palace had been timed for 4.30, but the procession was behind schedule. There had been the slightly delayed start. The marshals had had to slow the pace down because the horses began to slip on the rain-washed roads. There had even been points, like the incline up from Pall Mall to Piccadilly, where police and soldiers lining the route had broken ranks to put their shoulders to the wheels of coaches. As the State Coach swung round the Victoria Memorial to enter the Palace gates there was one TV camera so positioned that the Queen seemed to be well aware of its presence, and of the fact that her final smile and bow of the procession was to the 27 million people who were also watching her and were as much as everybody else, herself included, a part of the emotional phenomen-on of a coronation. As the State Coach swung into the Palace gates and then disappeared, the crowd surged against the arm-locked barriers of the police and flooded in a human tide up against the Palace railings. The shouts

Making the first of her balcony appearances to watch the flypast, the Queen was attended by her Maids of Honour and accompanied by (left to right) Prince Charles, Princess Anne, the Duke of Edinburgh, the Duke of Gloucester, Queen Elizabeth the Queen Mother, Princess Margaret, Prince Richard, Prince William, Prince Michael, the Duchess of Kent, Princess Alexandra and the Duke of Kent.

Troops came from all over the Commonwealth to take part in the coronation procession. Here Papuans, marching barelegged and without hats, form part of the Australian contingent.

Part of the 'Family Group' photograph taken at Buckingham Palace on the return from the Abbey and in which only Prince Charles seems unaware that this was a moment of recorded history.

of acclamation had changed to a great roar of 'We want the Queen' before she was even in the Palace.

Inside the Palace another stage was already set – for the official group and family photographs by Cecil Beaton that had to be taken while everybody was there, and in full costume, robes and trains. The crowd which wanted the Queen had to wait – not at her pleasure, but for other responsibilities to be fulfilled. The arrangement was that she would make her first balcony appearance, not so much in response to the insistent demands of the crowd, but to be there for the arranged RAF flypast. A tight-formation flypast had been prepared and the pilots from Wattisham and Horsham St Faith had thoroughly rehearsed not just that tight formation which had to be flown as a practised team, but contingency variations of it. During the Abbey service there had been a 'weather flight', and the pilot had had to report that unless the low cloud lifted a tight formation over London would be 'dicey'. Indeed the whole idea of a flight might have to be abandoned. Inevitably it had to be a last-minute decision. And with the 168 jets already airborne, that decision finally rested with Air Vice-Marshal Lord Bandon, the RAF executive controller stationed that afternoon on the roof of Buckingham Palace. The moment came when he lifted a telephone and said: 'I'm bringing them in!'

Then, at 5.40, the windows of the balcony opened and against a great roar of human voices the Queen, still crowned and wearing the Royal Robes, came out followed by the Duke of Edinburgh, Prince Charles and Princess Anne, the six maids of honour, the Queen Mother and Princess Margaret. And then the roar of the crowds was lost in the greater roar as the first wing of twenty-four Meteors came screaming overhead, tearing the low cloud apart, coming and vanishing in a moment made frightening by its abruptness and brevity in conditions of poor visibility, and followed by another, another, another, another, another and yet another crescendo of sound and a brief vision of black arrows hurtling across the cloud.

In all, the Queen was to make six balcony appearances for the crowds in the Mall, which were never less than 150,000 people. At seven o'clock Prince Charles and Princess Anne were allowed a last wave of their own from the third-storey window, on their way to bed. At 7.20, still wearing her crown, the Queen appeared on the balcony for the second time, now just with Prince Philip.

They came out again at 9.45, and this time the Prince was in a dinner jacket. It was now raining, it was dusk, and, here and there, there were umbrellas gleaming with black wetness in the dense crowd that was solid all the way down to Trafalgar Square. The sight obviously did not seem credible from the balcony. The television viewers, with a close-up of the balcony, were able to lip-read Philip's: 'This is marvellous, isn't it?' The Queen stepped forward. She pressed a switch. And then she was seen to clap her hands in delight, and to point down the Mall. She had unleashed upon London a river of gleaming light that challenged the brilliance of all the jewels there had been in the Abbey. The tall and graceful arches spanning the Mall blazed. The long rows of pennants and crowns flooded with light. The huge cypher over Admiralty Arch sprang to life. Nelson's Column leaped out of the darkness as the floodlights bathed it. The lights ran over the West End horizons and towards the distant City as searchlights tilted their probing fingers into the hurrying grey clouds. The cheering began to die down and became an utter silence as hidden loudspeakers began to relay the programme the BBC had timed to coincide with the switching on by the Queen of the coronation lights. In absolute quietness they listened to her coronation broadcast from Buckingham Palace to the Commonwealth.

When I spoke to you last, at Christmas, I asked you all, whatever your religion, to pray for me on the day of my Coronation – to pray that God would give me wisdom and strength to carry out the promises that I would then be making.

Throughout this memorable day I have been uplifted and sustained by the knowledge that your thoughts and prayers were with me. I have been aware all the time that my peoples, spread far and wide throughout every Continent and ocean in the world, were united to support me in the task to which I have now been dedicated with such solemnity.

Many thousands of you came to London from all parts of the Commonwealth and Empire to join the ceremony, but I have been conscious too of the millions of others who have shared in it by means of wireless or television in their homes.

All of you, near and far, have been united in one purpose. It is hard for me to find words in which to tell you of the strength which this knowledge has given me.

The ceremonies you have seen today are ancient, and some of their origins are veiled in the mists of the past. But their spirit and their meaning shine through the ages never, perhaps, more brightly than now.

I have in sincerity pledged myself to your service, as so many of you are pledged to mine. Throughout all my life and with all my heart I shall strive to be worthy of your trust.

In this resolve I have my husband to support me. He shares all my ideals and all my affection for you. Then, although my experience is so short and my task so new, I have in my parents and grandparents an example which I can follow with certainty and with confidence.

In West Berlin there was a
coronation march past of
British troops. Here
Russian and American
officers stood side by side
as the military band
played the British
National Anthem.

Coldstream Guards march
through a small street on
the outskirts of London.

CORONATION

There is also this. I have behind me not only the splendid traditions and the annals of more than a thousand years, but the living strength and majesty of the Commonwealth and Empire, of societies old and new, of lands and races different in history and origins but all, by God's will, united in spirit and in aim.

Therefore I am sure that this, my Coronation, is not the symbol of a power and a splendour that are gone, but a declaration of our hopes for the future, and for the years I may, by God's grace and mercy, be given to reign and serve you as your Queen.

I have been speaking of the vast regions and varied peoples to whom I owe my duty, but there has also sprung from our island home a theme of social and political thought which constitutes our message to the world, and through the changing generations had found acceptance both within and far beyond my realms.

Parliamentary institutions, with their free speech and respect for the rights of minorities, and the inspiration of a broad tolerance in thought and its expression – all this we conceive to be a precious part of our way of life and outlook.

During recent centuries, this message has been sustained and invigorated by the immense contribution, in language, literature and action, of the nations of our Commonwealth overseas. It gives expression, as I pray it always will, to living principles as sacred to the Crown and monarchy as to its many Parliaments and peoples.

I ask you now to cherish them – and practise them too. Then we can go forward together in peace, seeking justice and freedom for all men.

As this day draws to its close, I know that my abiding memory of it will be, not only the solemnity and beauty of the ceremony, but the inspiration of your loyalty and affection. I thank you all from a full heart. God bless you all.

She had, of course, said it all. The great crowd stood bareheaded in the rain, in continuing silence, as the national anthem was played. Then the Queen waved, and she and her husband began to go inside. And this time the crowd sang the national anthem, needing no accompanying music.

Now, on the South Bank, the firework display began with an opening royal salute of fifty-one maroons. Along 900 feet of the river-mirrored Thames embankment there were waterfalls of light, catherine wheels 100 feet across, pyrotechnic portraits of the Queen, of the Duke of Edinburgh, Prince Charles and Princess Anne. There were 3,900 rockets and 4,450 roman candles. London was a million stars, visible ten miles away in the finale of the coronation. But they would not go home. They would not leave the Mall. Again at 10.40 the Queen and Prince Philip conceded to the clamour and made a three-minute balcony appearance. And still the crowd before the Palace would not even begin to thin out.

At midnight, still radiant in a glittering white dress, ermine cape and diamond tiara, the Queen made her sixth appearance on the Palace balcony

PREVIOUS PAGE Immediately after the return from the Abbey, the first and immediate responsibility was the posing for the official group and family photographs. This was the formal picture of the Queen with her Maids of Honour and the Mistress of the Robes.

Street parties for children were casualties of the torrential rain of coronation day ... but there was always somewhere to take shelter. This picture is of some of the 305 children whose street party in Camberwell was transferred to the local school hall.

The magnificent firework display on the South Bank of the Thames: a fitting end to a unique day.

with Prince Philip. And then they began, at midnight, to sing *Auld Lang Syne*. It began with the crowds packed together in front of the Palace. It began simultaneously in Trafalgar Square, where the crowds had now become so dense that traffic was at a standstill, so dense that only an ambulance with clanging bell was managing to move at a crawl, so dense that a group of Morris dancers in full costume and with bells on their legs no longer found room to dance. And it seemed, if you were there, as if the whole of the capital had been orchestrated into the singing of *Auld Lang Syne*. And then at last they let her go, and the people began to go home or to hold their own individual coronation parties.

Epilogue

WHEN THE ARMY OF cleaners moved into the Abbey with their rubbish sacks and vacuum cleaners – which they did as soon as the last of the coronation congregation had gone, because the BBC television cameras were to show, that night, a reflective and retrospective midnight picture of the silent and deserted Abbey – it was a close-watched security operation.

Even a coronation Abbey congregation leaves a lot of litter, although the snack wrappings could be prestigiously identified as having come from Fortnum and Mason's or Harrods. The vacuum cleaner dust had to be sifted through, because at every coronation some diamonds, some emeralds, some rubies fall from their settings and their loss goes unnoticed. At the 1953 coronation a diamond necklace of very great value was found by the cleaners, before the Queen had even got back to the Palace – and it was not to be claimed for six weeks!

That incidental story of an aftermath of coronation day is typical of the kind of snapshot pictures without which no story of the event would be complete. But there are, of course, too many such stories, too varied in their nature, to arrange them into any pattern. There is no other way to tell them, except as snapshots – with the knowledge that no two albums of such snapshots would have the same contents.

In Korea on coronation day the British Commonwealth division artillery had instructions to fire a 101-gun coronation salute. The guns had to be pointed towards the enemy, but the barrage was plotted so that the shells would fall on 'dead ground'. The gunners were ordered: 'Be careful not to hit the Chinese.' 'We didn't', said a division officer later, 'think that it would be quite sporting to hit them with the Queen's salute.'

In Moscow Mr Molotov, Russian Foreign Minister, attended a coronation banquet at the British embassy. Mr Molotov proposed the toast of 'The Queen' – which was drunk in champagne.

In New York harbour on coronation morning there was pandemonium

The days and weeks following the coronation were crowded and eventful for the Queen. The first important occasion came on 9 June with the Coronation Thanksgiving Service. The Archbishop, Doctor Geoffrey Francis Fisher, preached the sermon and the lesson was read by Sir Winston Churchill. This photograph, taken during the service, shows, from right to left, the Queen, the Duke of Edinburgh, the Queen Mother, Princess Margaret, the Duke and Duchess of Gloucester, the Princess Royal, the Duchess of Kent, her son, the Duke of Kent and her daughter, Princess Alexandra.

Preceded by the Lord Mayor of London, Sir Rupert de la Bere, the Queen and the
Duke of Edinburgh leave St Paul's Cathedral after the Coronation Thanksgiving
Service.

as ships' hooters saluted the *Queen Elizabeth* coming in to dock. Theatre audiences in New York, Detroit and Boston spontaneously stood at the end of performances to the unfamiliar playing of the British national anthem. The *New York Post*'s banner headline simply said: 'HER DAY'. The *New York Mirror* managed to secure a picture of Prince Charles peeping out of a Buckingham Palace window, and they headlined this on their front page: 'PEEKA-BOO CHARLIE STEALS THE PALACE SHOW.' The first, very private and personal thing the Queen did on her return from the Abbey was to pin a coronation medal – the one struck for thousands of children all over the country – on to Prince Charles' chest. It was his first decoration and he wore it when he appeared on the Palace balcony with his parents for their first appearance at the RAF flypast.

In the Nevada desert, having been postponed by bad weather, the eleventh, the last and the greatest of a series of atomic blasts went off on coronation day. In Derby, 23,000 schoolchildren were presented with coronation silver spoons. In Warsaw the British ambassador, Sir Frank Sheppherd, whose embassy was in Stalin Avenue, displayed a twelve-foot picture of the 'Queen Elsbiette' on the building frontage and had it floodlit.

But the most original coronation decoration was claimed to be that in the small hamlet of Sutton, near Abinger in Surrey. A chestnut tree was still in full red blossom up to a height of fifteen feet. Then, by some freak of nature, the blossoms above were white. A local village boy climbed up right to the top of the tree to decorate it with blue streamers.

The coronation bonfire on the 500-foot Hillsborough Hill, outside Ilfracombe, caught fire on coronation eve, twenty-four hours ahead of schedule, and coronation day was spent in building a new bonfire. At Westleton, Suffolk, the Blyth Rural Council debated and approved a motion for the removal of a cow which was grazing by custom upon the village green. The cow was eating the coronation decorations. At ten o'clock on coronation night a rocket from Wolf Rock lighthouse in the Atlantic gave the signal for a chain of bonfires to be lit throughout Cornwall. Of the bonfires lit that night throughout the country from Land's End to John o' Groats, none had a closer connection with the coronation than the most northerly of them all. The John o' Groats bonfire was lit by a flaming branch carried in a five-foot-long torch-holder first used to light a coronation bonfire for Queen Victoria in 1838.

Every Welsh-born baby born on coronation day was given a silver spoon. At Symond's Yat in the Wye valley, they celebrated by roasting a 110-lb

The people of Windsor were well used to the presence of the Queen and her husband, but 13 June was a special occasion – a state visit. People crowded the pavements and the balconies and thousands lined the route from Slough to Windsor as the royal couple drove to Windsor Castle in an open coach.

A coronation visit to Scotland took place between 23 and 29 June. Here, in Edinburgh, where there was to be a National Service in St Giles' Cathedral, the residents of a close just off the Royal Mile are hanging up the paper garlands which might just be glimpsed by the Queen as she drove by.

The Queen and the Duke of Edinburgh with Lt Gen. Sir Colin M. Barber, Governor of Edinburgh Castle, during the royal visit to the Castle. The Duke is wearing the uniform of Colonel-in-Chief of the Cameron Highlanders.

The first great occasion after the coronation was the Review of the Fleet at Spithead, on 16 June, in which over 250 ships of all types and from many nations, including Russia, took part. This picture, taken aboard the Royal Yacht HMS *Surprise*, is of, left to right, Lt Gen. A. Gruenther (Chief of Staff of SHAPE), the Queen, Admiral Lynde McCormick (Supreme Allied Commander, Atlantic), Lord Ismay (Secretary General, NATO) and the Duke of Edinburgh.

OVERLEAF After a ninety-minute review of the ships anchored in line, the Queen dined that night aboard HMS *Vanguard*. And, for the occasion, the Fleet lit up with overall illuminations as a backcloth to a firework display.

Finnish reindeer. In the Shropshire and Derbyshire villages they were roasting deer, duck and chickens.

In York, the local harriers staged a torch race round the city's ancient Roman walls. At Ramsey, Isle of Man, sea cadets sent out a 'fire boat' from which blazed a Viking sea beacon. In the Peak District, on the borders of Staffordshire, Yorkshire, Nottinghamshire, Leicestershire and Cheshire, 100 hillside bonfires traced the county boundaries. A network of fire laced the kingdom that night. The biggest of the beacons was at Brocklesby in Lincolnshire where a towering pile of timber, thirty-five feet high, had been soaked in 100 gallons of old tractor oil.

The very first of the coronation day salutes was fired by a Royal Naval survey vessel, *Dampier*, at 12.10 am. It happened to be lying off Sandakan, North Borneo. In Ottawa, Canadian soldiers, sailors and airmen serving court-martial sentences were given a coronation amnesty and had their sentences reduced by one twelfth.

The 'quote of the day' came from a Royal Household staff member who said: 'The main concern at the Palace is that the horses will go slowly today, but that on Saturday *the horse* will go fast' – a reference to the Queen's entry in the Derby.

The most unusual of coronation gifts was one accepted by the Duke of Edinburgh from Alan Brockhurst of Marldon in Devon. This was a pint glass tankard on to which he had engraved the actual signatures of the leading personalities in science and aviation. For his work he had secured the signatures of Fleming, Watson-Watt, Whittle, Alcock and Brown, Stirling Moss and Geoff Duke.

The oddest coronation street party of all took place in a town called Shataukok, which consisted of one single street. Half the street celebrated with a distribution of tea and cakes and fireworks, while the other half looked on peacefully, or infiltrated to join in the celebrations. Half the single street of Shataukok was in British Territory, while the other half, across the frontier from Hongkong, was in Communist China.

Four seventeen-year-old youths were remanded in custody for a week at Fleetwood, Lancashire, on the day before the coronation. They were charged with shopbreaking. As they were taken down the magistrate asked the police to provide them, at his personal expense, with a packet of cigarettes each to smoke on coronation day.

Towards the end of coronation year, when it was all a matter now of memories, statistics, photographs and documented reports, two sociologists attempted an analysis of the 'social phenomenon of the coronation'. They

During her Scottish coronation visit, the Queen called on Mr and Mrs James Wilson, who lived in the Scottish Veterans' Garden City at Penilee, near Paisley. The plaque above the door of the gaily decorated home records the fact that it had been donated by the late Sir Harry Lauder.

made a joint report for the December issue of the *Sociological Review*, a publication of which very few of the millions who had watched and become emotionally involved in the event were likely to be aware.

One of the two authors was Professor Edward Shils, an American. The other was Michael Young, a member of the Labour party and a professed sceptic about the value of a monarchical system. The French philosopher and sociologist, Emile Durkheim, who died in 1917, had once said of such phenomena: 'There is no society which does not feel the need of upholding and reaffirming at regular intervals the collective sentiments and the collective ideas which make its unity and personality.' Shils and Young concurred with this view and said that, viewed objectively in retrospect, the coronation had been exactly this kind of ceremonial. 'We believe', said their report, 'that we are justified in interpreting it as a great act of national communion.' Twenty-five years later, nothing has happened to contradict or challenge the validity of that summing up.

Index

INDEX